Left: Full flat wash on skin; partial wash on Safari-inspired jumpsuit (Linda Bryant for F.O.B., Los Angeles). Right: Partial wash on skin; full flat wash on playsuit (Dorothy Schoelen, California). See Chapter 8, The Partial Wash in Color.

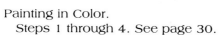

Painting in Color.
Steps 1 through 4. See page 30.

intermediate fashion design and water color illustration
second edition

MAXINE WESTERMAN

illustrated by the author and
Women's Wear Daily artists

FAIRCHILD PUBLICATIONS • NEW YORK

Standard Book Number: 87005-495-3

Library of Congress Catalog Card Number: 83-83401

Printed in the United States of America

introduction

This workbook is primarily intended for use as the second half of a course of study introduced in *Elementary Fashion Design and Trade Sketching: a workbook for the beginner.* Although it may be used by itself, it presupposes a rudimentary knowledge of fashion sketching and the basics of design.

Its purpose is twofold:

1. To continue on a more advanced level a discussion of the principles introduced in *Elementary Fashion Design and Trade Sketching.* While the elementary workbook concentrates on dress design, *Intermediate Fashion Design and Water Color Illustration* discusses other categories of apparel design, such as sportswear, children's wear, playclothes, beachwear, evening wear, sleepwear, loungewear, and suits and coats.

2. To introduce a simple step-by-step approach to water color painting. Included are basic color theory and the most popular illustrative painting techniques.

To derive the best results from this course of study, the work for each chapter should be done in the order of its presentation. Exercises are carefully planned to provide maximum growth through a series of steady progressions.

acknowledgments

The author wishes to acknowledge with thanks the help of Deborah Marquit, cover illustrator; Barbara Scholey, Book Designer and Olga Kontzias, Editor, Fairchild Publications.

With thanks to the following *Women's Wear Daily* artists: Pedro Barrios, Kenneth Paul Block, Stephen Cervantes, Dorothy Loverro, Steven Meisel, Robert Passantino, Catherine Clayton Purnell, Joel Resnicoff, Steven Stipelman, Glen Tunstull, Robert Young.

contents

UNIT 1
blouses

CHAPTER 1—DESIGNING BLOUSES

SOME PRACTICAL CONSIDERATIONS

Cost

Climate and Occasion

Age and Size

SOME BASIC CONSTRUCTIONS

The Shirtwaist

The Tuck-in

The Overblouse

THE CREATIVE APPROACH

EXERCISES 1, 2, AND 3

CHAPTER 2—PAINTING A FLAT WASH

SUPPLIES

PROCEDURE

1. Transferring A Drawing

2. Arranging A Work Space

3. Mixing A Gray Wash

EXERCISES 4, 5, AND 6

BUILDING SHADOWS ON THE FLAT WASH

PROCEDURE

EXERCISE 7

CHAPTER ONE
designing blouses

SOME PRACTICAL CONSIDERATIONS

Cost, climate and occasion, and age and size groupings are practical considerations which strongly influence the development of apparel design. These factors affect not only the design of blouses, but also of other types of manufactured ready-to-wear.

COST—The cost of manufacturing a garment is an important influence upon its design. Manufacturers produce for specific markets. For example, a manufacturer may sell his blouses to a chain of stores which retails merchandise at budget prices. His designer must therefore create a line of blouses which wholesales inexpensively, while at the same time providing a reasonable margin of profit to the manufacturer.

CLIMATE AND OCCASION—Climate and the occasion for which a blouse is purchased affect its styling. Will it be worn at work or in the evening? Beneath a suit or over a long skirt?

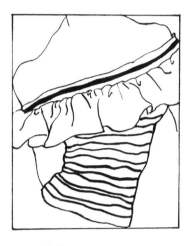

Summer Sport—Very casual polyester knit.

Is it for summer, winter, fall, or spring? Shall it have long sleeves or short; dark colors or pastels; lightweight fabric or heavy? Be décolleté or covered up? The thoughtful designer considers physical comfort and the function of a garment, as well as cost.

AGE AND SIZE—Age group and figure size are among the most crucial factors influencing design. The average designer works within a

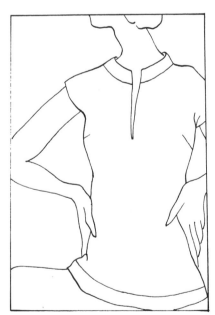

Budget Priced—Simple construction: two darts, no placket, no trimming.

Higher Priced—More complicated construction: collar, sleeves, cuffs, button-down front, pockets and tabs.

Classic Shirtwaist—Goes almost everywhere, all year-round.

2

particular category such as juniors, misses or women's, and each one requires an approach to design quite different from the others.

Above: Junior. Below: Misses and Women's.

SOME BASIC CONSTRUCTIONS

While blouses are as varied as the number of designers designing them, certain styles and types of construction are extremely popular, and frequently repeated. Within these basic patterns, changes occur primarily in the details of design (collars, yokes, sleeves, cuffs, closings, etc.); and in the types of trimming used (buttons, bows, seaming, stitching, ruffles, tucks, appliqué, embroidery, etc.).

The *shirtwaist,* the *tuck-in* and the *overblouse* are basic styles with somewhat standardized constructions. The development of wash-and-wear stretch knits, however, has revolutionized the blouse industry, eliminating the need for darts and closings which with other fabrics remain essential.

THE SHIRTWAIST

Tapered—Shaped by side seams. Styled after a man's ''body shirt'' of the Sixties.

Semi-fitted Stretch Knit—Bust fullness and shaped seams are not required.

Unfitted—Shoulder dart fullness converted into shirring at yoke.

3

THE TUCK-IN

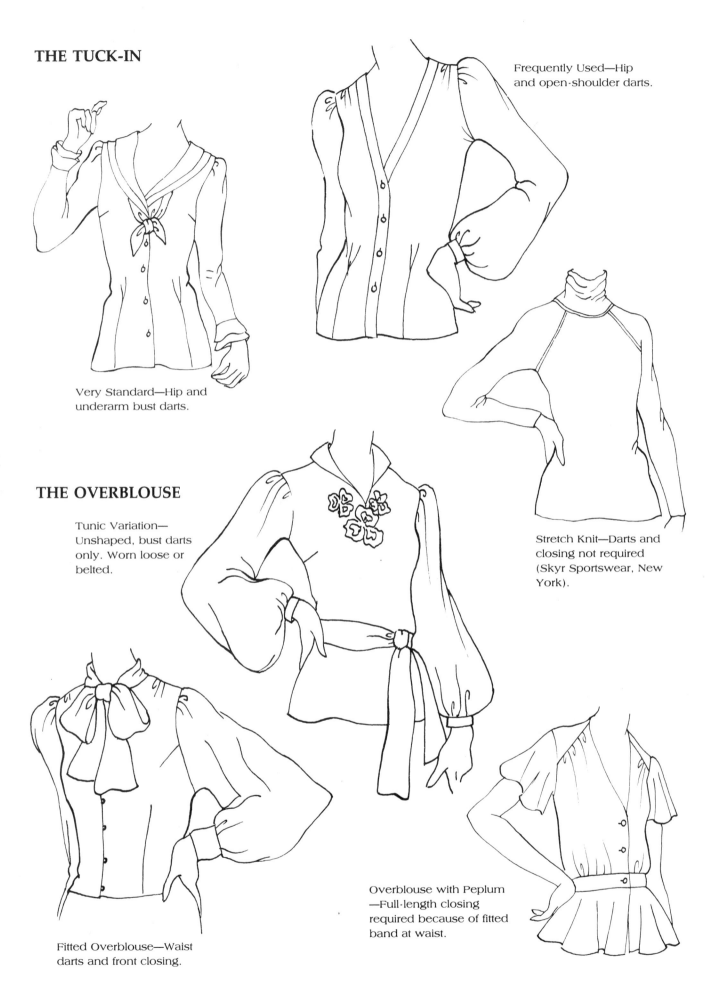

Frequently Used—Hip and open-shoulder darts.

Very Standard—Hip and underarm bust darts.

THE OVERBLOUSE

Tunic Variation—Unshaped, bust darts only. Worn loose or belted.

Stretch Knit—Darts and closing not required (Skyr Sportswear, New York).

Fitted Overblouse—Waist darts and front closing.

Overblouse with Peplum—Full-length closing required because of fitted band at waist.

4

THE CREATIVE APPROACH

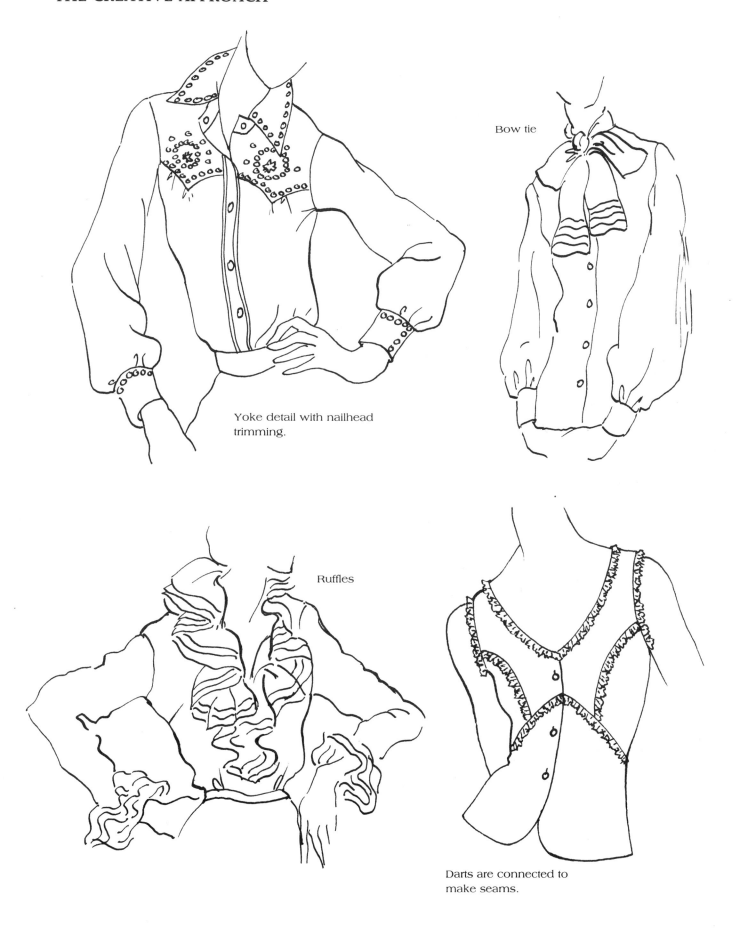

Bow tie

Yoke detail with nailhead trimming.

Ruffles

Darts are connected to make seams.

THE CREATIVE APPROACH

Historically inspired yoke, tucks, and sleeve detail.

Placket, tab and stitching detail (Regina Lewine).

Yoke, sleeve, and shirring detail (Regina Lewine).

Historically inspired collar-sleeve coordination.

THE CREATIVE APPROACH

Although certain blouse constructions are popular and commonly used, more novel creations result when a designer departs from the limitations of standard patterns. Connecting darts to create interesting seam arrangements, transforming darts into shirring, designing with yokes, referring to historical or other types of costume as a source or inspiration, and employing a variety of design elements (buttons, bows, ruffles, ties, tucking, piping, banding, seaming, stitching, etc.) are all part of a creative approach to designing blouses.

EXERCISE 1

Undress one thumbnail and five larger blouse figures. Develop the croquis. (See *Elementary Fashion Design and Trade Sketching*, pp. 21–26.)

EXERCISE 2

Design ten blouses on tracing paper over the thumbnail croqui. Vary your designs by utilizing some popular design elements such as collars, yokes, sleeves, cuffs, closings, buttons, seaming, stitching, ruffles, ties, tucks, appliqué, embroidery.

POINTS TO REMEMBER— ERRORS TO AVOID

1. Make certain that all the blouses can be put on and removed without difficulty. Except for stretch knits, fitted blouses require top to bottom closings—preferably in front.

2. Back closings are difficult to reach, while zippers can be bulky and impractical on lightweight fabrics.

3. Unfitted tunics may be pulled over the head, eliminating the need for top to bottom closings. High necklines, however, require neck plackets.

4. Bust fullness must be accounted for—either through the use of darts, seams or shirring. The five basic bust darts are the shoulder dart, the armhole dart, the underarm dart, the neckline dart, and the center-front dart. The French dart is used to remove bust and waist fullness simultaneously. (See *Elementary Fashion Design and Trade Sketching*, pp. 33–34.)

5. Waist darts or French darts will shape a blouse between the bust and waistline. Hip darts will shape it below the waistline. (See *Elementary Fashion Design and Trade Sketching*, pp. 35–37.)

EXERCISE 3

Select five of the ten designs and illustrate them on tracing paper over the remaining croquis. Set these drawings aside for Exercise 6 in Chapter 2.

CHAPTER TWO

painting a flat wash

SUPPLIES

Illustrating fashion with water colors requires the use of specific supplies. Although initially costly, these materials may last many years when properly cared for. If you started this course of study with *Elementary Fashion Design and Trade Sketching,* you already possess some of the supplies listed below.

1. A few number 2H drawing pencils or a lead holder and box of 2H leads.

   2H leads provide hard, crisp lines which do not smear when covered with paint.

2. A few number 2B drawing pencils or a lead holder and box of 2B leads.

   2B leads provide soft, dark lines ideally suited for the transference of drawings from tracing paper to water color paper (provided a light box or window are not available for this procedure).

3. A small portable pencil sharpener for regular pencils, or a special sharpener for lead holders.

4. A kneaded eraser.

   Kneaded erasers are gray in color and can be stretched and pulled like chewing gum. They leave no marks or debris, and will not remove the surface of water color paper.

5. A drawing board.

   Drawing boards are rectangular pieces of wood or masonite sold in varying sizes. The recommended size for the exercises in this textbook is 18 inches by 24 inches. Drawing boards are absolutely essential for water color painting, as will become clear when you commence work.

6. A drawing board clip.

   Special clips are made for drawing boards. They clip one or more layers of paper to the board, eliminating the need for push pins.

7. A roll of masking tape.

   Masking tape will fasten paper to any surface including wood or glass. It will not tear or mar the paper when removed, as will transparent tape.

8. Tracing paper.

   Tracing paper is a thin, transparent paper available in pads or packages. Preliminary drawings are made on tracing paper, from which they may then be transferred to water color paper.

9. Water color paper.

   Water color paper is made in many grades and weights, and has a wide price range. Shop around—find the price to suit your budget. Pads or "blocks" are less costly than individual sheets of paper. Select a medium weight paper which will not stretch or buckle when water is applied. Surface textures vary from smooth to very rough. A mildly textured surface is suitable for fashion rendering. An approximate size of 10 inches by 14 inches is recommended for the exercises in this book.

10. Water color brushes.

    The quality, size and price of brushes also varies greatly. Red sable is extremely durable, and well worth the extra investment. Brushes should cover a size range from very thin (for painting fine lines) to thick (for large washes). Start with numbers 0 or 1, and continue with numbers 2, 3, 4 and 5. If a larger brush is needed, then add a 6 or 7 to the collection.

    When purchasing brushes, test them by dipping them into water. The hairs should come to a closed point when wet, and not be loose or falling out. Never soak your brushes—remove them from water and stand them brush side up immediately after use. Soaking brushes loosens the glue, causing the hairs to fall out.

11. A water color set.

Large, elaborate paint sets are unnecessary, and tubes of paint expensive and impractical for fashion rendering. A small set of semi-soft cakes in a metal or plastic container is perfectly adequate. If it contains the primary colors red, blue and yellow; the secondary colors orange, green and purple; and black and brown, then nothing more is required.

12. A tube of Chinese White water color paint or a tube of white tempera paint for special painting techniques.

13. A water color palette.

A palette is a small white plastic or enamel tray, either rectangular or circular, with individual hollowed out spaces for mixing paints. Quite often the lid or cover of a paint set serves as a palette, but if it is attached to the set, or does not lie flat when open, a separate palette is preferable.

14. Two containers of water.

One for washing brushes, and one for thinning paint.

15. One package of absorbent blotters.

Absolutely essential. Blotters may be purchased from any stationery shop.

PROCEDURE

1. TRANSFERRING A DRAWING—You are now about to transfer the five blouse drawings made on tracing paper (see Chapter 1, Exercise 3) to a sheet of water color paper. There are three methods for this procedure:

METHOD 1. If you are fortunate enough to be in a classroom which contains a light box, you have at your disposal the fastest and simplest technique for transferring drawings.

Place the sheet of tracing paper with the blouse drawings on the glass of the light box, and cover it with a sheet of water color paper, both right side up. Switch on the light, and you will see right through the opaque water color paper to the drawings underneath. Trace them with 2H lead.

METHOD 2. You may simulate the effects of a light box by using an ordinary window in your home or classroom, provided it is daylight.

Place the sheet of tracing paper with the blouse drawings on it up against a window where there is plenty of light. Tape it to the window with masking tape, with the blank side against the window.

Put a sheet of water color paper on top of it, right side facing you, and tape that down also. You should be able to see your drawings through the water color paper. Trace them with 2H lead.

METHOD 3. This method should be used when neither a light box nor a window is available.

On the *back* of the tracing paper which contains your drawings, go over every line with soft, dark lead (2B).

Then place the tracing paper on *top* of a piece of water color paper, with the back side (and the 2B lines) facing down (touching the water color paper).

On the top side of the tracing paper, draw over all the lines again, using a hard lead (2H). The pressure of your pencil will transfer the soft 2B lines from the back of the tracing paper to the front of the water color paper.

Remove the tracing paper and set aside for further use.

Clean up any smudges on the water color paper with a kneaded eraser. Run the eraser lightly over the rest of the drawing to remove any excess lead, which may smear a bit when paint is applied.

2. ARRANGING A WORK SPACE—A systematic approach to painting promotes the best results. An uncluttered work space (table top or desk) with adequate lighting is the first requirement.

After arranging a work space, set out the following supplies: a paint set, a palette next to the paint set, two containers of water with a blotter beneath each, one extra blotter, and a container holding your brushes in an upright position.

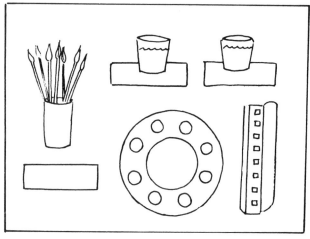

Arranging a work space

3. MIXING A GRAY WASH—Fill about one half of one of the cupped spaces in your palette with clean water. Wet a number 4 or 5 brush and slightly dampen the black paint in your paint set with it. Then dip the brush with the black paint on it into the clear water in the palette, turning the water gray.

Test the color on a scrap of water color paper—wait for it to dry. Water color paint lightens as it dries. If the color is very pale, continue to add black paint, a bit at a time, until you have a medium-gray wash.

10

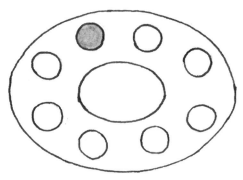

Mixing a gray wash

EXERCISE 4

Do not attempt to paint your blouse drawings just yet. Water color is extremely difficult to handle at first, so some practice painting is recommended. A well-painted flat wash is free of streaks and spots.

Fill a sheet of water color paper with two inch squares, and paint them with a medium-gray wash. Practice painting them until they are absolutely flat—that is, free of streaks and spots, and not spilling over the edges. Use the following procedure, which should give you good results after a number of trials.

STEP 1.   Place the drawing board with paper clipped to it in your lap, leaning against the table at a comfortable angle. Water color painting is done in an upright position, never flat on the table.

STEP 2.   Load your number 4 or 5 brush generously with the gray wash in the palette.

STEP 3.   Paint a stripe across the top of the square, moving from right to left. The brush should be so loaded that the area just painted will be dripping with small puddles along the bottom.

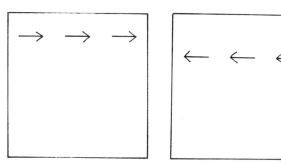

Steps 3 and 4

STEP 4. Very quickly load your brush again and paint a second layer just below the first, moving from left to right. Overlap the first layer about a quarter of an inch. The wet paint of the first layer will blend with the second, and no streaking should result.

NOTE: If the first layer of wash dries before the second is applied, streaks will form. The trick is to keep each layer of paint so wet that it blends into the next one before drying (and therefore streaking) can occur.

STEP 5. Continue loading your brush and painting down the square. At the end of the bottom row, a small puddle of paint will remain as you lift your brush. Dry the brush quickly on a blotter and place the tip of the brush into the puddle to soak it up.

EXERCISE 5

For the color gray, develop a value scale which goes from light to dark. Your ability to paint shadows will directly depend upon mastering this exercise.

STEP 1. Arrange a sheet of water color paper with two inch squares. Set up supplies. Fill one of the hollow spaces of your palette with clean water.

STEP 2. Mix a very light gray wash and paint the first square with it.

STEP 3. Add just a drop of black paint to the same wash to make it one value darker. Paint the second square.

STEP 4. Continue adding black paint to the original wash until all the squares are painted in progressively darker values (see illustration).

Step 5

Exercise 5, Step 4

11

EXERCISE 6

Paint the five blouses (from Exercise 3) on water color paper with a flat wash. Do not use color. Limit the paintings to values of gray.

Select a small brush and practice painting accented lines. Accented lines vary from light to dark and thin to thick. (For a detailed review of accenting, see *Elementary Fashion Design and Trade Sketching*, p. 64.)

Complete only two of the five blouses with accented brush lines. Set aside the remaining three for building shadows in Exercise 7.

BUILDING SHADOWS ON THE FLAT WASH

For the purpose of fashion rendering, a detailed or overly realistic approach to shading is unnecessary. Our goal is to illustrate a garment in a simple but attractive manner, so that construction and design are the most obvious features. Shadows add a touch of three-dimensionality to an illustration, enhancing its general appeal. Demonstrated in the illustration is a step-by-step approach to painting shadows, suggested for further exercises.

Blouse is painted with a flat wash. Skin and hair are painted with a partial wash. Accented lines vary from light to dark and thin to thick.

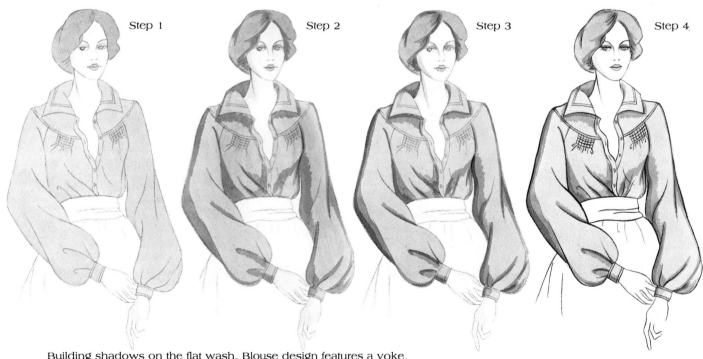

Step 1   Step 2   Step 3   Step 4

Building shadows on the flat wash. Blouse design features a yoke, smocking, and coordinated collar and cuff details (Helene Sidel).

12

PROCEDURE

STEP 1. Mix a batch of gray wash and use it to cover the garment with a flat wash. Let it dry thoroughly before continuing.

STEP 2. Add a small amount of black paint to the same batch of wash, making it slightly darker.

Paint a large area of shadow. If you are working with a three-quarter view figure, concentrate the shading on its large side.

Shadows fall in folds, under collars, beneath the bust, and may be applied wherever shaping is desired.

Use a loaded brush and try to paint the shadow in one continuous movement from top to bottom. If reloading becomes necessary, do it quickly so that no drying occurs before you reach the bottom of the illustration.

Shadows have shapes. Develop the shadow so that its shape is interesting as well as functional.

Let the shadow dry thoroughly before continuing.

STEP 3. Add a small amount of black paint to the same batch of wash, making it slightly darker than the first shadow color.

Paint a second layer of shadow. It should be smaller and darker than the first, and shaped slightly differently.

(For a detailed review of the application of shadows, see *Elementary Fashion Design and Trade Sketching,* Unit 10.)

STEP 4. Mix a small amount of black wash for the accented brush lines.

Sample your small brushes and select one which is flexible enough to render a very fine to medium line

Finish the painting with accented brush lines. They should be thicker and darker where shadows fall.

NOTE: Never brush up and back over an area already painted while the paint is still wet—the first application of water color paint should be the finished statement. Otherwise, the area which is painted over will streak and be darker than the rest.

EXERCISE 7

Paint the three remaining blouses set aside for this exercise (from Exercise 6) with a flat wash and built-up shadows. Do not use color. Limit these paintings to values of gray. Follow the procedure just outlined.

notes

UNIT 2 active sportswear

tennis

FACTORS TO CONSIDER

Tennis, one of the fastest growing sports in the United States in the Seventies, is less demanding of the novice designer than some other active sports. Ski wear, for example, requires a highly technical approach to design. Fit, warmth without weight, details of construction which provide flexibility and stretch in areas of tension, and a knowledge of special weather fabrics are just some of the factors to be considered. Designing for tennis, however, calls primarily for creative flair and a limited knowledge of the sport. The basic considerations are fit, comfort, and practicality.

FIT—Tennis involves a great deal of body movement, especially of the arms and legs. For this reason, traditional tennis wear has been designed with sleeveless tops and skirts for women, rather than shorts. The advent of stretch knits, however, has very positively affected the industry, encouraging a much wider range of styling.

Contemporary design has seen the inclusion of jumpsuits, apron wraps, bib-front dresses, short overalls, athletic shorts with T-shirt tops, sun dresses, and bodysuits with snap-on skirts.

COMFORT—Comfort is closely related to fit. A garment which neither pulls nor restrains the

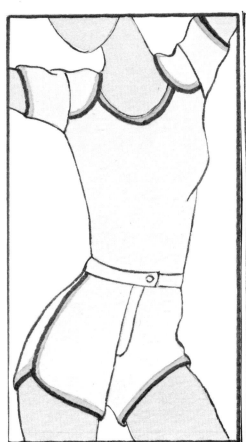

Tennis design made with a blend of cotton and Lycra spandex having stretch, "breathability," and fit (Danskin).

Terry cloth shorts and cover-up with contrasting tank top T-shirt, collar, and cuffs (Willie Smith for Paprika, New York).

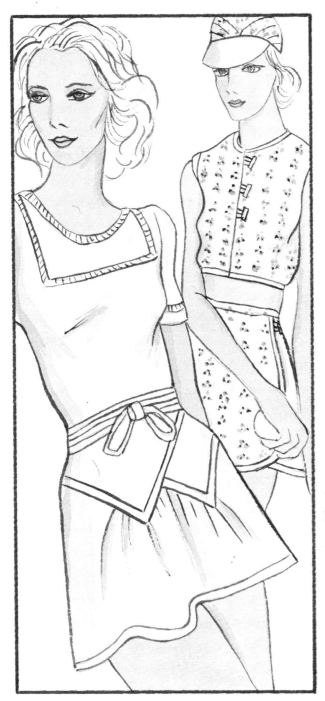

Left: Yoked, wrapped skirt in cotton duck teamed with a white cotton T-shirt (Geoffrey Beene for Geoffrey Beene Tennis, New York). Right: White polyester and cotton eyelet lined in pink (Lily's Boutique of Beverly Hills).

body in motion has an advantage. Fabric particularly conditions comfort. Where sunshine, action, and perspiration combine, then flexibility, absorbability, and breathability (the circulation of air) are preferred fabric features.

PRACTICALITY—A good set of tennis can be hard on an outfit, which usually comes off the body quite damp. It is seldom, if ever, worn again before washing. The serious tennis

White pull-on skirt with matching body suit in cotton and polyester knit (Catalina, Los Angeles).

player owns more than one change and alternates them frequently. For that reason, easy-care fabrics are the rule.

Cotton knits and cotton-backed polyester knits that are absorbent, terry cloth fabrics that stretch for action, and the woven drip-dry fabrics that hang neatly and straight are particularly popular because they fulfill the basic requirements for good fit, comfort, and practicality.

COOL WEATHER TENNIS—THE WARM-UP SUIT

Warm-up suits are designed to fulfill the tennis player's need for outdoor, cool weather outfits with versatility and style. The more practical suits can be used for other sports as well as tennis—jogging, cycling, golfing, and just plain lounging.

Popular fabrics include sweatshirt knits, terry cloth, velour, sweater knits, polyester blends, acrylics, shiny wet-look nylons, and corduroy. Frequently applied design details are hoods, zippers, drawstring waistlines, knitted cuffs, and side stripes. But as with other trendy wearing apparel, fabric and details of design change from season to season.

EXERCISE 8

Design five tennis outfits on tracing paper over a thumbnail croqui. Select one and redraw it on tracing paper over a full-size croqui (between 10 and 12 inches if your water color paper is 14 to 15 inches high). Set this drawing aside for Chapter 4, Exercise 9.

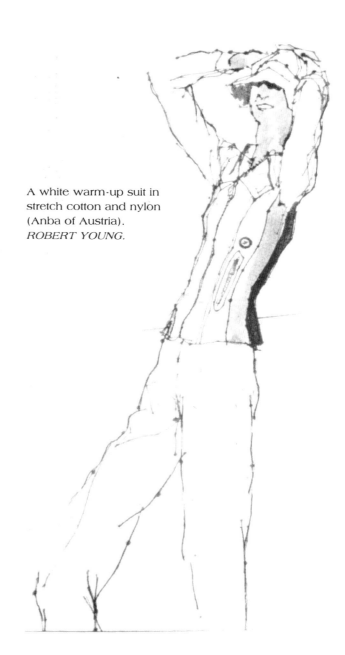

A white warm-up suit in stretch cotton and nylon (Anba of Austria). *ROBERT YOUNG.*

Reversible Kodel polyester and cotton warm-up suit (Berk-Ace, New York). *CATHERINE CLAYTON.*

notes

the partial wash

The partial wash is a fast, effective, and simple method of illustrating fashion. Its popularity and frequent employment by professional and student illustrators recommend it for careful study and further use.

The step-by-step partial wash is illustrated in these white pull-on terry cloth shorts with red and white elastic waistband topped by a white cotton knit T-shirt (Monika Tilley for Profile, New York).

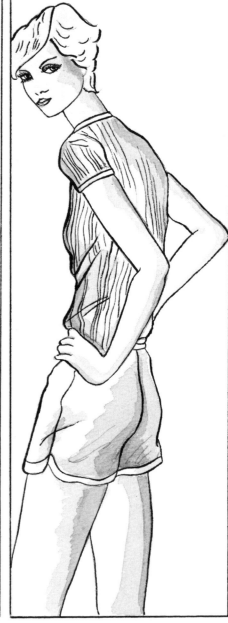

Step 1. Paint a large area with the first wash.

Step 2. Paint a layer of shadow, smaller and darker than the first wash.

Step 3. Finish with accented brush lines.

PROCEDURE

STEP 1. Mix a gray wash. If using a three-quarter view figure, apply an area of paint to the large side of the body.

Use a loaded brush and work from top to bottom. Avoid backtracking, or "painting over."

Shape this partial wash so that it gives form both to the body and the garment.

STEP 2. Add a small amount of black paint to the gray wash in your palette, making it a few values darker.

Wait for the first application of paint to dry thoroughly.

Paint a layer of shadow on top of the first application of wash, but much smaller and with a different shape.

STEP 3. Wait for the second application of paint to dry thoroughly.

Complete the illustration with accented brush lines. Paint them thicker and darker in areas of shadow.

EXERCISE 9

Transfer the tennis outfit on tracing paper (from Chapter 3, Exercise 8) to a sheet of water color paper. Illustrate it with a partial wash. Follow the painting procedure just outlined.

notes

UNIT 3 children's wear

CHAPTER FIVE
infants through teens

SIZE RANGES

The physical proportions of children change radically as they mature from infants into adolescents. Because of these changes, manufacturers divide children's wear into size ranges, which are related to the age of a child.

Infants—from birth through eighteen months.

Toddlers—eighteen months to about three years.

Children—about three to six to seven years.

Girls—about seven to ten years. (At this point, boys' wear assumes the same styling and production methods as men's wear.)

Sub-teens—about ten to thirteen years.

FACTORS TO CONSIDER

Children's apparel should satisfy the needs of children at various stages of development. While teenagers are mature enough to express their own likes and dislikes, comforts and discomforts, younger children are dependent upon the choices made by others. It is therefore the responsibility of the designer of children's wear to consider health and comfort as well as appearance and practicality. Specific factors to be considered in the design of children's wear vary with age and size.

THE INFANT—The skin of a newborn child is very tender, and extremely sensitive to the discomforts caused by wetness, temperature changes, and the weight of heavy covering. Infants' wear should therefore be light, soft, warm, and washable. Materials touching the skin are best blended with cotton for increased absorbency, while stretch fabrics permit movement and some room for growth. For mothers, easy-care, no-iron features are primary considerations.

The Infant

THE TODDLER—Babies who have learned to walk are toddlers. Their clothes should provide freedom of movement and protection against falls and scrapes. Overalls and knitted shirts are very popular. Outerwear should be lightweight and warm, as is the case with washable quilted nylon jackets and snowsuits.

The Toddler

24

THE PRE-SCHOOL CHILD—Average pre-schoolers are physically active, able to adequately dress themselves by the age of five (provided clothes are easy to manipulate with simple closings), and have distinct preferences (usually for bright colors and soft textures). Large armholes, front closings, uncomplicated fasteners, easy-care fabrics, and color and design are the factors to consider.

The Pre-School Child

MIDDLE CHILDHOOD—The seven- to ten-year old is often involved in numerous activities. Sportswear, especially for active sports, is much in demand. Girls of this age reject design features of younger groups (such as puffed sleeves and smocking), preferring clothes which more closely resemble junior styling with a touch of sophistication.

SUB-TEENS—The adolescent girl has a need to identify with her peer group, and to stand apart from the older generation. "Her clothes must be different, reflecting the taste of her own age group . . . For the designer, it is a constantly exciting challenge to keep up with young fads and fancies within the framework of fashion and good taste."*

Sub-Teens

Middle Childhood

* Hilde Jaffe, *Children's Wear Design* (New York, 1972), p. 22. (A comprehensive and authoritative book recommended for further study; the source for most of the information contained in this chapter.)

SOURCES OF INSPIRATION

The approach to children's wear design is primarily functional, accommodating the specific needs of children. There is, however, room for tremendous diversity. Some of the sources to which designers turn for their inspiration include trimming, current fashion trends, historical and folk costume, and children's literature.

Appliquéd Coordinates (Just Girls, New York).

Popular trimmings for children's wear include eyelet, braid, ribbon, lace, embroidery, appliqué, emblems, patches, fancy stitching, smocking, and edging.

SEASONAL CATEGORIES

Children's wear is divided into seasonal categories, each of which contains special types of clothing. These categories are defined as follows:

BACK-TO-SCHOOL—Includes tailored fall dresses and separates, jackets and coats. Fabrics are primarily washable wool blends, corduroys, and cottons.

HOLIDAY OR SPECIAL PARTY CLOTHES—These are more fanciful and less practical than most other children's wear. Velveteen and sheer fabrics are particularly popular.

SPRING CLOTHES—Includes coats and suits, dress and coat ensembles in light, bright colors; mostly in wool blends.

SUMMER WEAR—Primarily playclothes and separates.

EXERCISE 10

Select two seasonal categories of clothing and two age and size groups with which to work. For example: snowsuits for toddlers, holiday dresses for middle childhood.

Develop one croqui for each of the age groups you have chosen.

On tracing paper over the croquis, design five outfits for each group (ten all together).

Select two designs and transfer them from tracing paper to water color paper. Set aside for painting with color (see *Chapter 6, Exercise 12*).

notes

CHAPTER SIX

painting in color

BASIC COLOR THEORY

Color theory is a complex, technical field of study. But for the purpose of designing and illustrating fashion, a combination of innate good taste and a knowledge of basic color theory should provide the essential ingredients for creative expression in color.

PRIMARY AND SECONDARY COLORS—The primary or basic colors are red, yellow, and blue. When properly selected and mixed, they produce the secondary colors orange, green, and purple.

Red + Yellow = Orange
Yellow + Blue = Green
Blue + Red = Purple

TERTIARY COLORS—Some colors result from the combination of three others. For example, red, yellow, and black in the proper proportions produce brown. Brown can also be mixed from blue and orange (orange con-tains the two primary colors red and yellow).

Red + Yellow + Black = Brown
Blue + Orange = Brown

BLACK AND WHITE—Black and white are colors at opposite extremes of the scale of grays. White is the ultimate limit of a series of tints, while black is the ultimate limit of a series of shades.

TINTS AND SHADES—A tint is a color diluted with white, or in the case of water color paint, diluted with water. It has less than the maximum "chroma," or color saturation. Pink is a tint of red.

A shade is a color with black added to it. Navy blue is a shade of blue.

COMPLEMENTARY COLORS—Complementary colors are found opposite each other on the color wheel. Red and green are complements; yellow and purple are complements;

A scale of grays; black and white are colors at opposite extremes.

No Contrast   Some Contrast   Bold Contrast

blue and orange are complements.

When complementary colors are placed next to each other, they intensify each other. Each color looks brighter, and seems to vibrate. That is why one rarely finds a garment of green and red together in equal proportions. The effect would be somewhat shocking and hard on the eyes. But complementary colors used in small areas, such as on a scarf, will serve to call attention to that area.

However, if complements are changed by the addition of white, black or some other color, then the impact they have upon each other is lessened. Pink next to green is not as intense a combination as red next to green.

MIXING GRAY FROM COMPLEMENTS—When complementary colors are mixed together *in equal proportions,* they neutralize, or cancel each other out, producing gray. Gray may therefore be mixed either from black and white (or in the case of water color paint by diluting black with water), or from two complementary colors.

Red and Green are complements:
Red + Green = Gray.
Yellow and Purple are complements:
Yellow + Purple = Gray.
Blue and Orange are complements:
Blue + Orange = Gray.

VALUE AND CONTRAST—Value refers to the amount of light or dark in a color. Colors can have light, medium, or dark values. Tints have medium to light values; shades have medium to dark values.

Colors are often selected for the amount of contrast provided by their values. For example: two light colors adjacent to each other provide little contrast; a light color next to a medium one provides some contrast; whereas light next to dark colors create bold contrasts.

That is why one rarely, if ever, finds a cos-

tume designed with black and navy blue. This is an extreme example of minimal contrast.

INTENSITY—Intensity refers to the strength of a color. A pure, full strength (or fully saturated) primary or secondary color, undiluted by the addition of white or black, would have maximum intensity. In the case of water color paint, the less water diluting a color, the more intense it will be.

MIXING SHADOW COLORS

Shadows are darker and duller than the colors upon which they fall—they are less intense. There are two simple ways to mix shadow colors:

1. Add a color's complement to it. For example, to mix a red shadow, add a bit of green.

2. Add black or brown. For example: for yellow, orange, and red—add brown; for blue, green, and purple—add black.

PROCEDURE

SKIN COLOR—Skin color can be produced in a number of ways:

1. By diluting brown;
2. By mixing red and orange with a touch of brown and diluting with water;
3. By mixing orange with a touch of red and diluting with water.

ACCENTED BRUSH LINES—Accented brush lines on the skin are brown. On the garment they are a very dark value of the color of the garment.

If the garment is red, yellow, or orange, add brown to produce the color of the accented lines.

If the garment is blue, green, or purple, add

29

black to produced the color of the accented lines.

STEP 1. Paint the skin and hair with flat washes. Let them dry thoroughly. Save the washes for mixing shadow colors.

Paint the garment with a flat wash. Let it dry thoroughly. Save the wash for mixing shadow colors.

STEP 2. Darken the skin wash very slightly (one value only) and paint a layer of shadow on the skin.

Darken the hair wash a few values and paint some shadows on the hair.

While the skin and hair are drying, darken the garment wash and paint a layer of shadow on the garment.

STEP 3. When the first layers of shadow are thoroughly dry, darken the washes again and paint a second layer of shadow on the skin, hair, and garment.

STEP 4. When thoroughly dry, paint the details on the face. Finish the hair with fine brush lines.

Complete the painting with accented brush lines.

EXERCISE 11

Mix the color gray from a combination of two complementary colors. (See ''Complementary Colors,'' page 28.)

1. Draw six, two-inch squares on water color paper. Select a primary color and paint the first square with it.

2. For each successive square, add a little more of that color's complement, until the next to last square has turned a very dark gray.

3. To paint the last square a medium value neutral gray, dilute the dark gray with water.

EXERCISE 12

Paint the children's wear drawings set aside for this exercise (from *Chapter 5, Exercise 10*) on water color paper. Follow the outlined painting procedure discussed on page 29.

Painting in Color.
Steps 1 through 4. For color rendering turn to inside front cover.

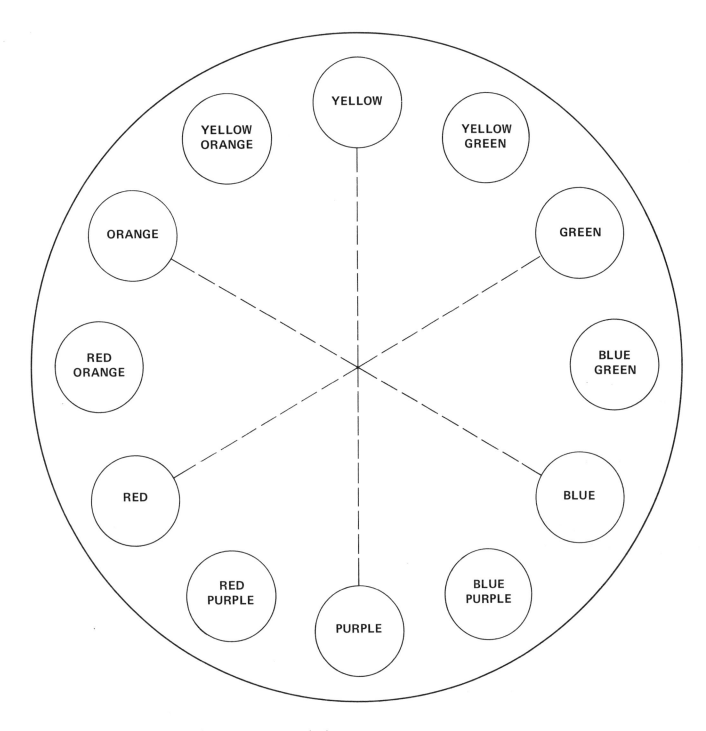

Color Wheel. For color rendering turn to inside front cover.

notes

UNIT 4
playclothes

designing playclothes

TYPES OF PLAYCLOTHES

Playclothes are generally conceived as a special category of summer sportswear. Traditionally included among the more popular articles of playclothes are playsuits, rompers, sun dresses, shorts, culottes, pants, tops, matching sets, overalls, and jumpsuits.

FACTORS TO CONSIDER

For the country girl, playclothes are frequently made for summer-round living. For the city dweller, they are more often designed for vacation wear.

As playclothes are worn during a wide range of activities—such as hiking, cycling,

Left: Diaper-wrap black cotton (Cardinalli Barber for Malibu Media, California). Center: T-shirt romper in white cotton knit (San Francisco Shirt Works, California). Right: Boxer shorts and halter top in blue cotton (Branch Division of Joshua Tree, California). *STEVEN MEISEL.*

Left: White eyelet jumpsuit
(Kay Unger for St. Gillian,
New York). Center: Harem
jumpsuit in raspberry
crinkled cotton (Cathy
Hardwick, New York).
Right: Yellow cotton
jumpsuit (Gil Aimbez for
Genre, New York).
STEVEN MEISEL.

picnicking, boating, gardening, sightseeing, and just plain lazing around—the primary factors to consider in their design are *comfort, practicality, variety, versatility,* and *good looks.*

Easy fit, durable but carefree fabrics, and smart styling are the essential features of playclothes.

EXERCISE 13

On tracing paper over a thumbnail croqui, design ten playclothes outfits. Select the best two and draw them on tracing paper over full-size croquis.

Transfer the drawings to water color paper and set them aside for painting (see *Chapter 8, Exercises 14* and *15*).

Matching shirt, shorts, and vest in khaki cotton (Bill Kaiserman for Rafael, New York).

notes

the partial wash in color

The partial wash may be applied in color as well as with values of gray. It is frequently combined with a full wash, either shaded or unshaded, for enhanced visual appeal.

Left: Full flat wash on skin; partial wash on Safari-inspired jumpsuit (Linda Bryant for F.O.B., Los Angeles). Right: Partial wash on skin; full flat wash on playsuit (Dorothy Schoelen, California). For color rendering turn to inside front cover.

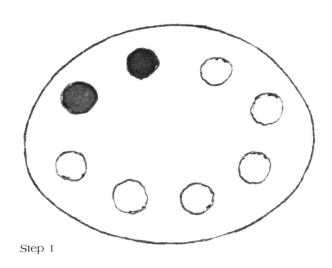

Step 1

PROCEDURE

STEP 1. Mix two batches of wash, the second a few values darker than the first.

STEP 2. Paint a large area with the first wash.

STEP 3. Paint a layer of shadow, smaller and darker than the first wash.

STEP 4. Finish with accented brush lines.

EXERCISE 14

Paint one of the drawings set aside for this exercise (see *Chapter 7, Exercise 13*) as follows:

With a partial wash on the skin and hair, and a full, flat unshaded wash on the garment. Use color.

EXERCISE 15

Paint another of the drawings (see *Chapter 7, Exercise 13*) set aside as follows:

With a full, flat unshaded wash on the skin and hair, and a partial wash on the garment. Use color.

Step 2

Step 3

Step 4

CHAPTER NINE
stripes

The all-seam, no-dart construction of this sundress personifies the ideal stripe design (Juanita Kempe for Sassy Lassy, California). *DOROTHY LOVERRO.*

DESIGNING WITH STRIPES

There are two methods of designing with stripes. The first is to design a garment and afterwards to choose a striped fabric for its construction. The second method involves the selection of a striped fabric, out of which evolves a specific design for that particular fabric. This is the preferred technique for designing with stripes.

The ideal design utilizes the stripe as its most important feature. Construction and design are worked around the pattern of that stripe. The placement of seams is carefully planned to create a definite effect. Darts are avoided, if possible, where they cut into and destroy the rhythm of the striped pattern.

ILLUSTRATING STRIPES— POINTS TO REMEMBER

1. Stripes are almost always printed in the direction of the warp (vertical or lengthwise yarn) of a fabric, and run parallel to the selvage. Therefore, when a pattern is pinned to a piece of striped fabric, the stripes and the straight grain (warp threads) are parallel.

2. When illustrating stripes, keep them equidistant from each other. They should not come together or spread apart. Note the A-line skirt illustrations. On one, the stripes are running parallel. On the other, the stripes follow the shape of the skirt—a natural and frequently made mistake for beginning illustrators, but definitely not correct.

3. Shirring is an exception to the general rule that stripes are illustrated parallel to each other. Shirring pulls the stripes together so that they appear to be closer to each other at the top, while spreading apart at the bottom.

4. Stripes will also "come together" and lose

their parallel appearance when pulled in by a dart or seam.

5. Horizontal stripes on shirred fabric run parallel to the hemline.

6. When folds appear in a garment, the stripes will sometimes break, and then pick up again over the fold.

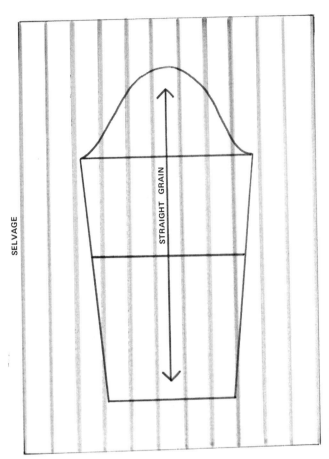

SELVAGE

STRAIGHT GRAIN

Basic sleeve pattern on striped fabric. Grainline of sleeve runs parallel to stripes.

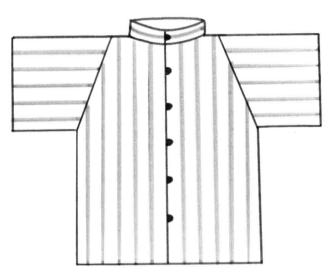

All the pieces of this jacket are cut on the straight grain, which accounts for the direction of the stripes on the sleeves and on the mandarin collar.

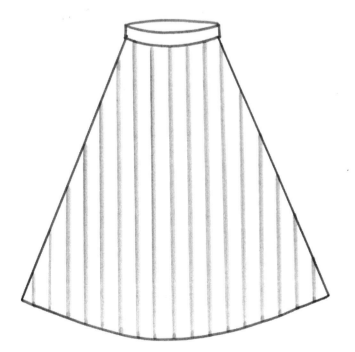

Left: Correct—Stripes remain parallel. Right: Incorrect—Stripes come together at the top and spread out at the bottom.

41

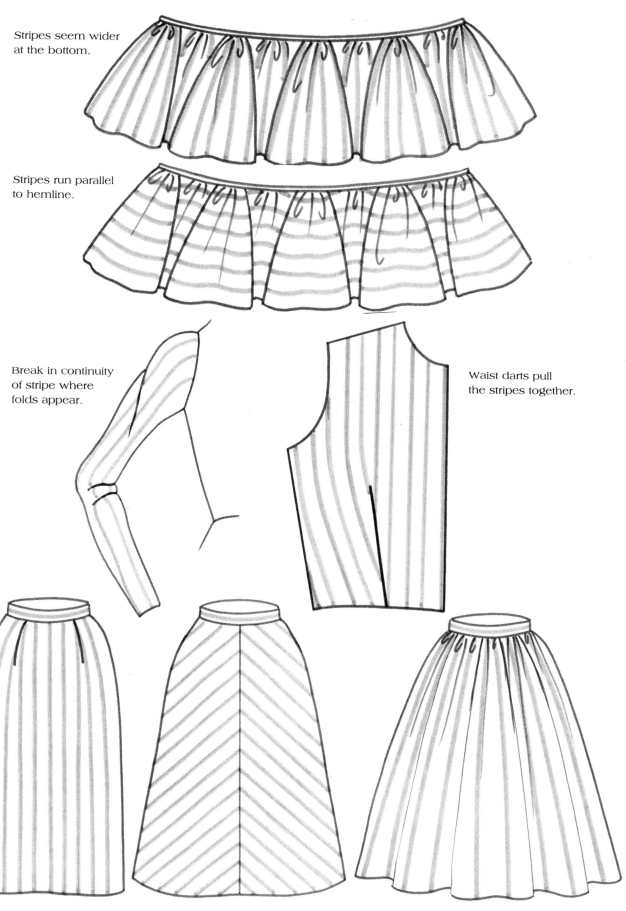

Stripes seem wider at the bottom.

Stripes run parallel to hemline.

Break in continuity of stripe where folds appear.

Waist darts pull the stripes together.

Straight skirt with hip darts.

A-line skirt with center seam.

Gathered skirt with vertical stripes.

42

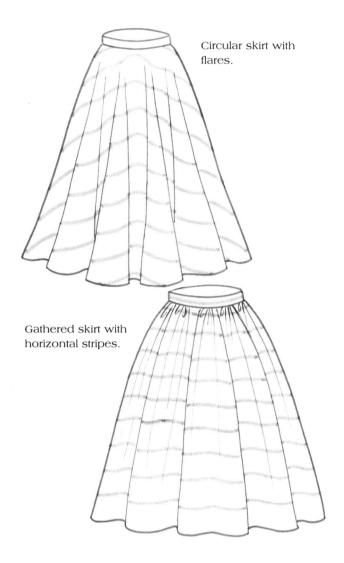

Circular skirt with flares.

Gathered skirt with horizontal stripes.

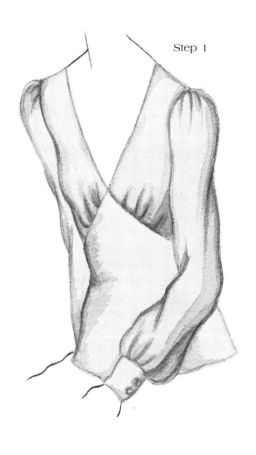

Step 1

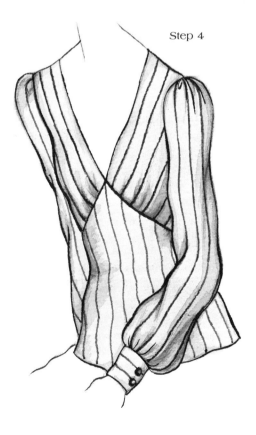

Step 4

PAINTING STRIPES

STEP 1. Using a flat wash, paint the background color of the fabric.

STEP 2. Build up the shadows.

STEP 3. Work out the stripe design in pencil, and then paint it.

STEP 4. Finish with accented brush lines.

EXERCISE 16

On tracing paper over a thumbnail croqui, work up five designs for striped fabric. Include a sun dress, a jumpsuit, and other types of playclothes.

EXERCISE 17

Select the best design from *Exercise 16* and transfer it (full size) to a sheet of water color paper. Paint it in color with a full, flat wash and built-up shadows. Follow the procedure just outlined.

White ribbon-banded seersucker sundress (Gil Aimbez for Genre, New York). Partial illustration techniques using Procedure II. *ROBERT YOUNG.*

ILLUSTRATING SEERSUCKER

PROCEDURE I—Work out a stripe pattern. Connect the empty spaces between each stripe with curved lines. These lines indicate puckers in the fabric.

PROCEDURE II—Work out a stripe pattern with very light pencil lines. Fill in the spaces between the stripes with pucker lines. Erase the pencil lines when the illustration is dry.

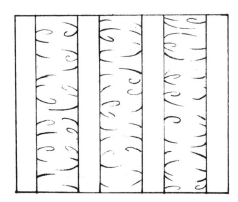

Procedure I

Procedure II

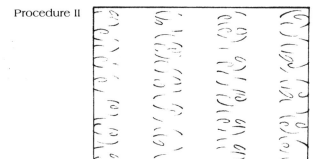

EXERCISE 18

Select another stripe design from *Exercise 16* and transfer it (full size) to a sheet of water color paper.

Paint a partial wash in tones of gray. Do not use color. Use either Procedure I or Procedure II to finish the illustration.

Note: If painting in color is preferred, follow the procedure outlined on page 43. Pucker lines are painted the color of a dark shadow. For example, if the seersucker is pale blue, the pucker lines should be a somewhat darker and duller blue.

notes

notes

UNIT 5
sportswear

CHAPTER TEN
designing sportswear

TYPES OF SPORTSWEAR

Sportswear is the most highly diversified category of women's clothing. Skirts, vests, jackets, matching coordinates, blouses, knit tops, shorts, jeans, pants, jumpers, jumpsuits, playclothes, sun dresses, and a variety of other types of apparel may all be classified as sportswear.

Because of this great diversity, there are no hard and fast rules for designing sportswear.

A top may be purchased for its delicately ruffled feminine appeal, while blue jeans fulfill a more practical purpose.

POPULAR DESIGN ELEMENTS

There are, however, a number of design elements frequently employed by sportswear designers which have proved consistently popular. These include belts, buckles, tabs, cuffs, buttons, novelty pockets, saddle and

Left: Squared-neck top and matching boxer shorts (B.K. & Co.). Center: Matching outfit features black buttons, tabs, and stitching on gold cotton vest; pockets, buckled belt, a zip-front closing, and front and back pleats on skirt (Lawrence Rich for Hangups, New York). Right: Red and white striped buckled vest with matching front-pleated skirt (Lloyd Greenleaf and Carmen Lodico for Foxey, New York). *ROBERT PASSANTINO.*

Knee length, bib-front ''painter's pants'' (Ms. Lee). *ROBERT YOUNG.*

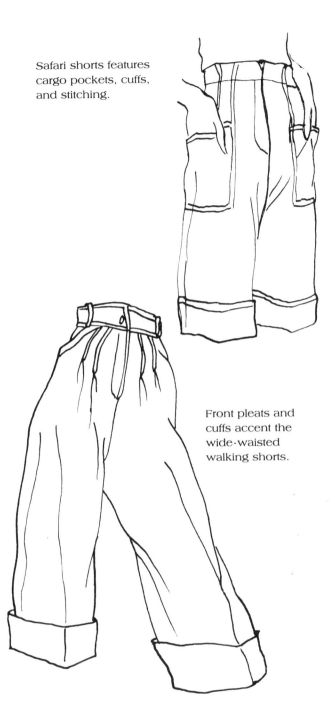

Safari shorts features cargo pockets, cuffs, and stitching.

Front pleats and cuffs accent the wide-waisted walking shorts.

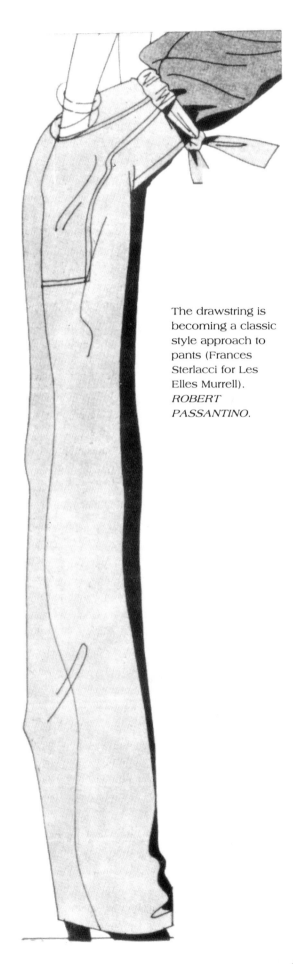

The drawstring is becoming a classic style approach to pants (Frances Sterlacci for Les Elles Murrell). *ROBERT PASSANTINO.*

top stitching, plackets with zip-front details, ties, yokes, drawstring details, pleats, wrap-around and culotte cuts, plus many others.

PANTS

Contemporary pants show a variety of lengths and design details—knee, mid-calf, above-the-knee, and ankle lengths; clam diggers, knickers, jodhpurs, elongated culottes, harem pants, pegged pants, and jumpsuits. Popular details include belts, yolks, cuffs, novelty pockets, drawstring ties, front pleats, and saddle stitching.

MATCHING SEPARATES

Matching separates have always been the special province of sportswear designers. The basic classics are still skirts and shirts, slacks, blazers, and city suits. Tunics topping pants, and safari jackets with walking shorts exemplify the trendy styling which enjoys great popularity for a limited span of time, until the fashion is revived.

SKIRTS

Traditional skirts have been pleated, gored, flared, gathered, belted, buckled, pocketed, and stitched. Contemporary skirts are also being wrapped around, side-buttoned, tie-belted, sashed, flounced, and aproned. They are often color coordinated with "mix-and-match" tops.

Butcher coat with matching pants (Bern Conrad for Irka). *ROBERT PASSANTINO.*

Drawstring-waisted pantsuit with novelty pockets and mid-calf "pirate's pants" (Jean Wallrapp for Glenora). *ROBERT PASSANTINO.*

Tunic-topped pants (Don Simonelli, New York). *JOEL RESNICOFF.*

A classic white duck blazer and a poplin jacket (Dana Cote d'Azur, New York). *ROBERT YOUNG.*

Top stitching and initialed cargo pockets detail a beige cotton skirt (Barbara Colvin at Liz Carlson, Los Angeles). Matching T-shirt is heat transfer printed. *STEPHEN CERVANTES.*

EXERCISE 19

On tracing paper over a thumbnail croqui, design the following:

1. Three "back-to-school" articles of sportswear. Include some of these details: novelty pockets, cuffs, collars, tabs, belts, stitching, and pleats.

2. Three coordinated pants outfits for fall and winter. Include some of the following: yokes, novelty buttons, pockets, saddle stitching, and drawstring details.

3. Three summer pants with mix-and-match interchangeable tops. Include plackets with zip-front details, and a decorative motif on at least one top.

4. Three pieces of sportswear showing an ethnic influence. Use either contemporary or historical folk costume as a source of inspiration.

EXERCISE 20

Select two designs from *Exercise 19* and transfer them (full size) to a sheet of water color paper. Paint one with a flat wash and built-up shadows. Use a partial wash in color for the other.

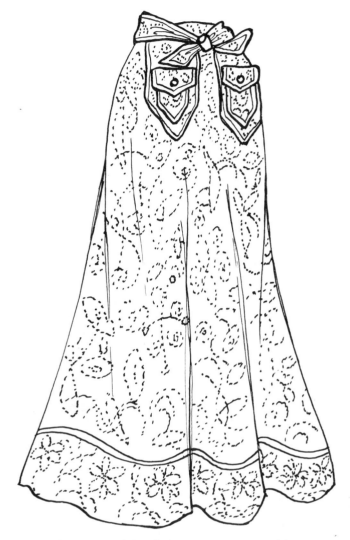

Floral-printed dirndl skirt sports a removable, double-pocketed sash (Jeanne Campbell for Sportwhirl, New York).

CHAPTER ELEVEN
checks and plaids

ILLUSTRATING CHECKS—PRINTED FABRIC LOOK

STEP 1. Draw vertical and horizontal lines to form squares.

STEP 2. Color the alternating squares.

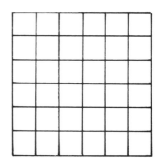

Printed Fabric Look: Steps 1 and 2.

ILLUSTRATING CHECKS—WOVEN FABRIC LOOK

STEP 1. Draw vertical and horizontal lines to form squares separated by bars.

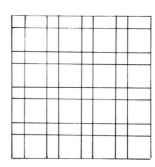

Woven Fabric Look: Steps 1 and 2.

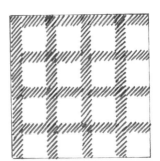

Woven Fabric Look: Steps 3 and 4.

STEP 2. Fill in the alternating horizontal bars with slanted lines.

STEP 3. Fill in the alternating vertical bars with slanted lines.

STEP 4. Color in the squares formed by the overlapping bars.

ON THE GARMENT (A-LINE DART, SIDE VIEW)

STEP 1. Vertical lines are drawn as stripes.

STEP 2. Horizontal lines are also drawn as stripes. Keep them at right angles to the verticals so that they form approximate squares.

STEP 3. Alternating squares are colored in.

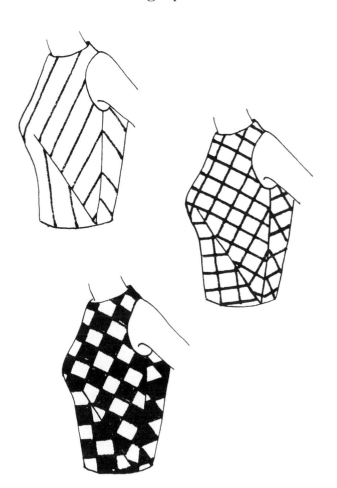

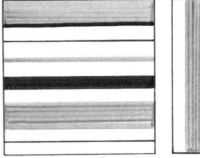

Step 1

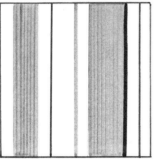

Step 2

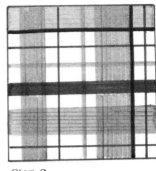

Step 3

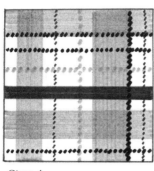

Step 4

ILLUSTRATING PLAIDS

There are many plaid pattern variations, as is also the case with checks. For our purposes, a simple technique for illustrating plaids will suffice.

STEP 1. Design a horizontal pattern of alternating bands and stripes.

STEP 2. Design a vertical pattern of alternating bands and stripes.

STEP 3. Put them together.

STEP 4. For a woven look, draw some of the lines as short, separate strokes.

ON THE GARMENT (PANTS AND VEST)

STEP 1. Block in the vertical pattern as you would a stripe. Vertical lines on pants follow the warp threads (straight grain) of the fabric.

STEP 2. Block in the horizontal pattern at right angles to the vertical lines. Horizontal lines on pants run parallel to the hemline.

ON THE GARMENT (PLEATED SKIRT)

STEP 1. Prepare the drawing showing pleats clearly separated.

STEP 2. Develop the vertical pattern following (or running parallel to) the warp threads (straight grain) of the fabric.

STEP 3. Develop the horizontal pattern at approximate right angles to the vertical. Horizontal lines follow the direction of the hemline.

On the Garment (Pants and Vest): Steps 1 and 2.

55

EXERCISE 21

Work out a series of plaid swatches on water color paper, in values of gray as well as in color. Select one gray and one colored swatch for *Exercises 22* and *23*.

EXERCISE 22

Select one of your sportswear designs from *Exercise 19* and transfer it (full size) to water color paper. Sketch in one of the plaid patterns.

In values of gray, paint as follows:

Use a flat wash with built-up shadows on the skin;

Use a flat wash without shadows on the garment.

EXERCISE 23

Select a second sketch from *Exercise 19* and repeat the procedure in *Exercise 22,* but finish the painting in color.

On the Garment (Pleated Skirt):
Step 1, Step 2, and Step 3.

56

notes

notes

UNIT 6
beachwear

CHAPTER TWELVE
designing beachwear: swimsuits and cover-ups

FACTORS TO CONSIDER

Beachwear, of all the many categories of feminine apparel, is one of the most challenging to the designer. Whereas a good deal of outerwear is purchased primarily for its appearance, beachwear should also satisfy the prerequisites of perfect fit, total comfort (stretchability, breathability, dryability), durability, and practicality. And last but not least, a swimsuit which fails to flatter its wearer will unquestionably be bypassed for another.

The following quotation from an advertisement by Malibu demonstrates just some of the factors (primarily of construction) considered by Malibu's designers:

Know that the high spandex content—75% nylon/25% spandex—gives that sensational second skin fit.

Know that the adjustable tie-bra is really adjustable, not just a decoration. . . .

Know that the waistband is set with a wide elastic band—one inch to keep bikini bulges down. And it's cover stitched not by one needle, but two, for greater give.

Also know that the legs are shirred in the back and flat in the front so the fit is true and smooth.*

DESIGNERS' COMMENTS

American designers are very much aware of the psychological processes affecting the selection of a swimsuit. Oleg Cassini, designing for Waterclothes, believes in maximizing a woman's natural assets.

Some designers would like to camouflage a woman, but I never believe in tampering with a woman's body . . . the swimsuit should be an envelope to the body—a second skin. A lot of designers like to flatten the

chest, but a girl shouldn't be considered vulgar if she shows a large chest.*

Donald Brooks takes a decidedly more sexual approach:

Some of my things are as close to total nudity as you can get. Girls who have well-conditioned bodies have no compunction about revealing themselves.*

But Brooks admits that his Maidenform market is limited to specific customers—the trim little sizes six to twelve.

POPULAR SWIMSUIT SILHOUETTES

Swimsuit fashions have changed radically throughout the years—from knee-length bottoms to the barest "string"; from knitted woolens to lightweight, fast-drying synthetics. Of the many styles which briefly occupied the limelight, only a few have made a lasting impression, being as popular today as when they first appeared. Among this group of classic silhouettes are the *maillot* and the *bikini*.

Two other styles—the *dressmaker* and the *hip-rider*—have also persisted in popularity. This is due to the fact that they cater to women either with special figure problems, or with a degree of modesty. In addition, a very practical marketing innovation of the Seventies has further accommodated the woman who is not a standard bust and hip size. Two-piece swimsuits are now available in the "intimate apparel" section of many department stores, where matching tops and bottoms are sold separately—permitting the purchase of one suit with different bra and brief sizes. A growing tendency to color-coordinate tops and bottoms, rather than match the printed fabric, also broadens the range from which to choose, to "mix-and-match."

* WWD, 11/12/75, p. 36.

* WWD, 11/12/75, p. 50.

THE MAILLOT—A one-piece swimsuit with-out a skirt, form-fitting and usually backless. It has been popular since the 1930's, when it was either knitted or constructed of jersey.

Contemporary maillots are most often made of synthetic blends of nylon and span-dex, which are lightweight, flexible, and fast drying.

THE BIKINI—A very brief two-piece swimsuit with a bra-type top, and pants cut below the navel, traditionally narrow at the sides. It originated with the famous French designer Jacques Heim, who introduced it to Paris in 1946. Its popularity has grown with time, and there are as many versions of the bikini as pebbles on the beach—including its variation in the middle Seventies, the ''string.''

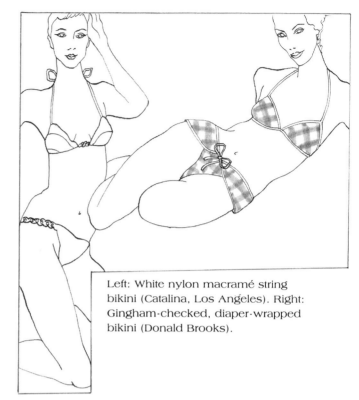

Left: White nylon macramé string bikini (Catalina, Los Angeles). Right: Gingham-checked, diaper-wrapped bikini (Donald Brooks).

Left: Forest green nylon and spandex wrapped effect (Elizabeth Stewart, Los Angeles). Right: Black polyester with cut-out top and sling neckline (Jer Sea, New York). *CATHERINE CLAYTON.*

Halter swim dress in black and white dotted Lycra spandex with a set-in midriff (Ethel Rogers, Gantner). *ROBERT YOUNG.*

Antron and Lycra spandex bikini with matching fringed shawl in Antron nylon (Jantzen). *ROBERT YOUNG.*

THE DRESSMAKER—A one-piece swimsuit with an attached skirt, and usually includes a

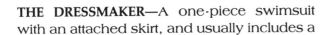
The Hip-Rider

sturdy, built-in bra. It is most often worn by the mature woman, but in fact can easily oblige a variety of figure problems.

THE HIP-RIDER—A two-piece suit with either low-slung pants or a skirt that exposes the navel. It became quite popular in the 1960's, when its compact-styling combined the best features of the bikini with the more conservative aspects of the dressmaker. For the female of any age with or without a weight problem, this silhouette comes as a special blessing. Exposing plenty of skin to the sun, it simultaneously covers unsightly bulges.

QUESTIONS TO CONSIDER

Consider and discuss the following questions:

1. Would a zipper closing affect the construction, appearance or comfort of a swimsuit? If so, how?

2. Can a dressmaker swimsuit be designed

without a zipper? If so, how easily can it go on and off the body?

3. Is it possible to avoid a back closing on a bra-top? How? What are the advantages and disadvantages of a front-closing bra-top?

COVER-UPS

Beachwear cover-ups include, among others, skirts, tunics, jumpsuits, rompers, capes, shawls, wrap-around sarongs, robes and jackets, full-length T-shirts, big tops, and caftans.

Favorite fabrics are terry cloth, transparent cottons and synthetics, crinkly cottons, stretch knits, slinky jersey, batik, and floral prints. But fabric preferences change from year to year. The important aspect of a cover-up remains the same—it serves a purpose, and must be functional as well as fashionable.

EXERCISE 24

On tracing paper over a thumbnail croqui, design five swimsuits for any size or age group, plus three dressmaker suits for the mature figure.

Select two designs, including one of the dressmakers, and transfer them (full size) to water color paper. Set aside for painting with a wet wash (see *Chapter 13, Exercise 26*).

EXERCISE 25

On tracing paper over a thumbnail croqui, design five beachwear cover-ups, some of which would be appropriate for printed fabrics.

Select one for a print illustration, and transfer it (full size) to water color paper. Set aside for painting (see *Chapter 14, Exercise 28*).

CHAPTER THIRTEEN
the wet wash

The wet wash differs from the painting techniques demonstrated in previous chapters in several ways:

FIRST—When painting a flat wash with built-up shadows (see Chapter 2, page 8), each layer of wash must dry thoroughly before the next one is applied. With a wet wash, however, shadows are brushed in while the first application of paint is still damp, causing a blending of the two colors.

SECOND—There is only one layer of shadow color used with a wet wash, as compared with the two or more applied when building shadows on a flat wash.

THIRD—There are also differences in the appearance of the finished product. The wet wash is a faster, freer technique giving rise to a more casual rendering, as opposed to the finely detailed results obtained from building shadows on a flat wash. When time is limited and a looser look preferred, the wet wash may be substituted satisfactorily for other painting techniques.

FOURTH—Finally, a wet wash must be applied with great speed and accuracy. Consequently, it is only after considerable practice that desired results are yielded with ease.

PROCEDURE

STEP 1. Set up a work table with all supplies within easy reach—two containers of clean water, a clean palette, assorted brushes, paints, blotters, and a finished drawing mounted on a drawing board.

STEP 2. Mix two batches of wash—one for the skin color and a second for the skin shadow. The second wash should be considerably darker than the first, because it becomes lighter as it blends into the skin color.

STEP 3. Apply the first wash. Start at the top and work your way down the figure, painting the skin very rapidly.

Steps 3, 4, 5, and 6

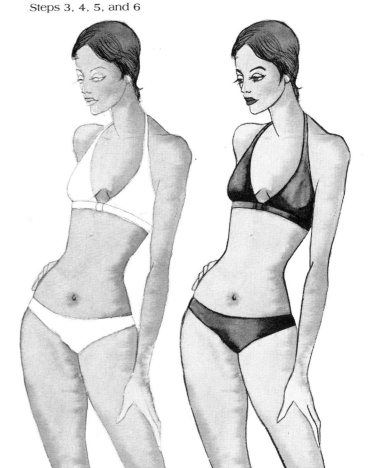

Step 2

64

STEP 4. While the paint you have just applied is still damp, apply the shadow color. Start at the top and work your way down the figure, painting very rapidly.

STEP 5. When the skin painting is completely dry, repeat the same procedure for the garment. Mix two batches of wash—one for the swimsuit and a second for its shadow. Apply the first wash, and while still damp paint the shadow.

STEP 6. When the entire painting is dry, finish with accented brush lines.

EXERCISE 26

Using a wet wash, paint the two swimsuit designs on water color paper set aside for this exercise (see *Chapter 12, Exercise 24*).

CHAPTER FOURTEEN
illustrating prints

THE WET WASH TECHNIQUE

The wet wash technique is one of a number of methods used for illustrating prints. It involves the application of color brushed on a wet background, resulting in a soft and blended look, with colors and shapes that "run" together. This is often combined with a hard-edged print pattern overlaying the muted background, which is rendered when the underlying painting is dry.

COLOR SCHEMES

The number of color combinations available for designing prints is practically unlimited. Three types of color schemes, however, appear with consistent regularity. These are the monochromatic, analogous, and complementary color schemes.

MONOCHROMATIC—This color scheme makes use of the tints and shades of a single

Monochromatic

color. Beige, tan, and brown are monochromatic colors, just as light blue, medium blue, and navy blue are also monochromatic.

ANALOGOUS—Analogous colors are found next to each other on the color wheel, and are

Monochromatic technique used in this African inspired jumpsuit—a cross between a sundress and wrapped-leg (Gil Aimbez). *PEDRO BARRIOS.*

related because they share a color in common. Blue, blue-green, and green are analogous colors because they all contain some blue (green is a mixture of blue and yellow).

COMPLEMENTARY—Complementary colors are found opposite each other on the color wheel. Green is the complement of red; orange the complement of blue; yellow the complement of purple.

PROCEDURE

STEP 1. Work out a number of rough sketches which repeat a print pattern at regular intervals. Select one for practice painting.

STEP 2. Mix three batches of wash—one for the background color, a second for the print pattern, and a third for the superimposed line work. Mix the first two washes darker than the desired value of the finished color, as they fade while drying.

STEP 3. Brush the area to be painted with clear water.

STEP 4. Brush the background color over the water.

STEP 5. While the background is still damp, brush in the print pattern with the second wash. This will more or less spread out and blend into the background, depending upon how wet the background is. The dryer the background, the less the second application of paint will spread.

STEP 6. When the first two washes are completely dry, paint the superimposed pattern with the third wash.

EXERCISE 27

Work out some rough sketches which repeat a pattern at regular intervals. Select a few for practice painting.

Following the outlined procedure, practice painting prints until satisfactory results are obtained.

EXERCISE 28

Using a wet wash on both skin and garment,

illustrate a print on the beachwear cover-up design set aside for this exercise (see *Chapter 12, Exercise 25*).

notes

UNIT 7
dresses

CHAPTER FIFTEEN
designing dresses

Dresses are the most staple category of feminine apparel. As ancient as the history of fashion itself, they promise to remain an essential part of every woman's wardrobe. Styles change, hemlines move up and down, fabrics come and go, but dresses stay. This is due to their tremendous versatility—a versatility which carries through each hour of the day and season of the year.

SEASONAL LINES

Spring, summer, fall, winter, and "holiday" are the seasonal lines which determine basic differences in fabric and styling. Fall and winter dresses are warm and cozy, showing a preference for darker colors and knitted or napped fabrics. While fall and winter styles and fabrics tend to run together, other lines show clear-cut differences. Holiday dresses, designed primarily for the Christmas-New Year season, are particularly decorative, making use of lush fabrics (velvet, lamé, taffeta, chiffon, satin, etc.) and gay trimmings (sequins, beading, etc.). Spring is a transitional season, with spring lines bridging the gap between winter and summer. Summer lines are bright and fresh, with white, pastels, florals, and ethnic prints particularly popular; and black a year-round favorite.

FACTORS TO CONSIDER

In addition to a consideration of climate and

Schiffli embroidery and chantilly lace trim a white cotton lawn two-piece dress with blouson top (Ma Chemise, California). *JOEL RESNICOFF.*

Multipurpose dress in Super Suede works with or without a belt; or with a skirt or turtleneck underneath for extra layering (Mary Martin, Los Angeles). *DOROTHY LOVERRO.*

season, the function for which a dress is purchased is an important factor affecting its design. The occasional dress is versatile enough to wear through both a working day and an evening out, but most dresses are more suitable for one purpose than another.

Further considerations are those which pertain to all categories of feminine apparel—age and size range, plus cost. Junior dresses differ from those designed for the mature figure; and the wholesale price range of a manufacturer's line will determine the quality and amount of fabric, trimming, and detailed workmanship.

Belle Saunders, a seasoned New York designer specializing in dresses for the mature figure, describes her primary goals as:

1. The creation of a classic look which retains its fashionability;
2. A fit that flatters;
3. A price that meets the average woman's budget.

POPULAR DESIGN ELEMENTS

There is no limit to the diversity of styling found in dresses. Traditionally popular design elements are collars, sleeves, tucking,

The "special occasion" dress: Wide-sleeved, tie-dyed Japanese silk is wrapped with a matching obi tie (Masako Takahashi).

The "all-purpose" spring into summer dress in black crinkled cotton with red top-stitching (Hector Milian, New York). *JOEL RESNICOFF.*

pleating, seaming, stitching, shirring, smocking, bias cuts, and other novelty patterns; plus a host of trimmings ranging from jewelled buttons to braided belts, with almost anything in between.

SOURCES OF INSPIRATION

One of the greatest single sources of inspiration for the designer is ethnic costume. American Indian leather work and beading, Mexican and Far Eastern embroideries, Moroccan caftans, Persian pants, Russian peasant wear, African dashikis, Scotch plaids and kilts, and Islamic, Indonesian and South Sea Island prints are just some of the ethnic motifs found in contemporary dress design.

Designer Belle Saunders attributes the overwhelming success of this two-piece dress and jacket combination in crisp cotton and rayon plaid to a number of features: The box-pleated skirt stitched below the hip is slimming; the timeless bolero jacket is flattering to any size and makes the waist look small; and the price was right.

Elasticized smocking is the special design element featured in this floral-printed cotton jersey (Oscar de la Renta, New York). *ROBERT YOUNG.*

Tucking, a buttoned placket and square-necked yoke detail this two-piece dress (Denise L., Los Angeles). *ROBERT YOUNG.*

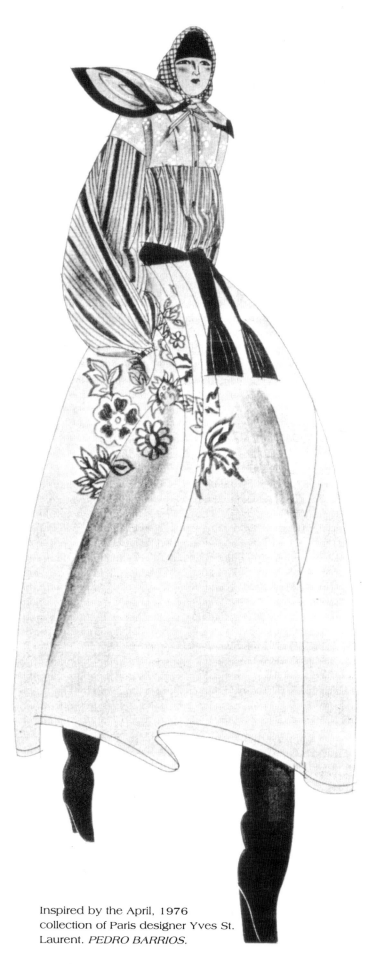

Inspired by the April, 1976
collection of Paris designer Yves St.
Laurent. *PEDRO BARRIOS.*

74

Other sources of inspiration are historical costume, fabric trimming; paintings, sculpture, and architecture; the theatre, ballet, and opera; movies, television, and books.

EXERCISE 29

Collect a batch of swatches of winter dress

Multi-colored, two-piece dress is bias cut with floating panels (DDDominick, New York). *ROBERT YOUNG.*

fabrics. These might include woolens, jerseys, corduroy, and other napped fabrics, plus a variety of synthetic and natural fiber blends.

Examine the swatches for their dressmaking qualities. For example: Does a particular fabric have body, or is it soft and ''drapeable?'' Does it stretch, or hang firmly? Is it too bulky for delicate details, or will it take to pleating, tucking, etc? These are the qualities which influence the direction of a dress design.

Select five swatches and design one fall-into-winter dress for each, keeping in mind an age and size range.

Select two dresses for illustration with any technique already learned, or one with which you prefer to experiment.

This sheer black version of the shirtdress has a snap-wrapped waist, stitched-down pleating, and top-stitched collar, cuffs, and pockets (Albert Nipon, New York). *JOEL RESNICOFF.*

CHAPTER SIXTEEN
illustrating eyelet

Eyelet embroidery is either patterned along a border, or has an overall design. Holes in the fabric are punched out and then overcast, with openings arranged in floral or conventional designs; and embroidery worked around the hole. It is found on transparent as well as opaque fabrics such as batiste, organdy, linen. Originally done by hand, eyelet is now produced on the Schiffli machine, which can embroider an entire width of fabric at one time, in simple or elaborate designs, and in many colors simultaneously.

Most eyelet fabrics are lightweight and crisp, making them ideally suited for dresses with full skirts, puffed sleeves, ruffles, flares, and shirring. This same crispness works against the use of eyelet for straight skirts and slacks, because the fabric tends to crease. Synthetic linen blends, however, are heavier but also more supple than organdy or batiste, so that a tailored look and smart seaming are preferred.

The simplest approach to illustration is to draw directly from a swatch of fabric. If, however, a sample is not available, then it is a simple matter to design a pattern.

BORDER PATTERN

Gathered ruffle with eyelet embroidery.

OVERALL PATTERN

EXERCISE 30

On tracing paper over a thumbnail croqui, de-sign five eyelet summer dresses for the junior size range five to fifteen, some of which would be appropriate for a lawn party or an afternoon wedding.

Select one and transfer it to water color paper. Use a full-size junior croqui.

PAINT IT AS FOLLOWS:

On the skin—Any technique.

On the garment—Use a flat wash with built-up shadows. Draw and then paint the eyelet pat-tern after building shadows, when the paint of the garment is thoroughly dry.

Finish with accented brush lines.

CHAPTER SEVENTEEN
illustrating sheers

Whether made of cotton, silk or synthetic yarns, all sheer fabrics have one thing in common, and that is their transparency. The degree of transparency varies from one fabric to another, just as the properties of weight, body, crispness or softness, and type of weave also vary. Batiste, muslin, and chiffon, for example, are very soft and drapeable; while organdy and dotted swiss are particularly crisp.

Illustration techniques, however, remain essentially the same for most sheers. Except for chiffon (dealt with in Chapter 23), the following procedure can be applied to all of the above mentioned fabrics.

PROCEDURE

STEP 1. Develop a finished pencil drawing on water color paper showing the skin and hinting at the undergarment (slip, camisole, lining, etc.); as well as the transparent overgarment.

STEP 2. Paint the skin and undergarment with a flat wash and built-up shadows.

STEP 3. When the underpainting is thoroughly dry (at least one hour after application—or even overnight), mix a thin wash for the transparent fabric. Brush the wash on very quickly without applying pressure.

STEP 4. When the first wash of the sheer fabric is thoroughly dry, mix a slightly darker second wash. Wherever there are folds in the garment so that a double or triple layer of sheer fabric is seen as a darker area, brush on the second wash, filling in the shapes of the folds.

STEP 5. Finish the sheer fabric with an ac-

Step 1

cented brush line only one value darker than the second wash. Keep the line thin and delicate. Sheer fabrics are not usually illustrated with sharp outlines.

To illustrate a printed sheer, follow the same procedure through *Step 5*. Then, when the painting is thoroughly dry, brush on the printed pattern.

The black and white rendering on page 80 is particularly effective because part of the arm and pant leg show through the transparent coat quite clearly.

EXERCISE 31

For the misses' size range six to sixteen, design five cocktail or afternoon dresses of sheer fabric (batiste, muslin, organdy, etc.).

Work from swatches of fabric wherever possible. Try to demonstrate the quality of the

Illustrating Sheers

Step 2

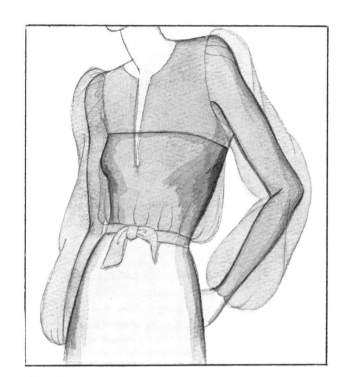

Step 3

Step 4

Step 5

Sleeveless jumpsuit with transparent-printed polyester chiffon coat (Jaconelli for Chiha, New York). *ROBERT YOUNG.*

fabric while sketching your design—crisp folds or soft, very transparent or semi-transparent, and so on.

Select one for illustration and paint it, following the procedure outlined.

notes

CHAPTER EIGHTEEN
illustrating prints

Step 1

Step 2

Step 3

THE FLAT WASH TECHNIQUE

Illustrating prints with a flat wash technique is a relatively simple exercise. Time and patience are the primary requirements.

STEP 1. Complete a detailed drawing.

STEP 2. Paint the background. Let it dry thoroughly.

STEP 3. Paint the remaining parts with their respective colors.

Because of the time it takes to illustrate an entire printed garment, some artists prefer to render a partial print rather than an overall design (see illustration on next page). Both partial and overall print renderings are frequently accompanied by a swatch of fabric.

The partial print is usually applied as one would apply a partial wash—to one side of the figure, in areas where shadows tend to fall.

EXERCISE 32

Collect some swatches of printed fabrics. Select one for illustration. Draw and then paint it as a swatch.

EXERCISE 33

For the women's size range thirty-eight to forty, design five daytime spring dresses. Include some two-piece dresses with jackets.

Select two for illustration. Transfer them (full size) to water color paper. Illustrate one with a partial print accompanied by a painted swatch.

EXERCISE 34

Illustrate the second dress (from Exercise 33) with an overall pattern, accompanied by an actual swatch of fabric pasted to the background.

Reproduced from a fabric design
of Wullschleger (New York).

Notice in the illustration the break in the print wherever it meets a fold or seam in the garment. Ungaro dresses from Sonia Knapp textile designs for Fournier (Paris). *KENNETH PAUL BLOCK.*

84

notes

notes

UNIT 8 evening wear

designing evening wear

A successfully rooted, middle-class society with plenty of leisure time and the means to enjoy it has gradually changed the concept of evening wear. The elegant ball gown, encrusted and bedecked with glitter of every kind—and the hours of laborious handwork attending it—still exists for the elite clientele of haute couture.

But the average American woman with both the ambition and opportunity to lead a stimulating and diversified life, demands a wardrobe which accommodates her many roles. Consequently, evening wear can be casual as well as formal; panted as well as skirted; practical as well as lovely; warm as

Black chiffon with silver sequins, designed by Koos van den Akker for the Empress of Iran. *STEVEN MEISEL.*

Lean and simple evening wear is designer Cathy Hardwick's specialty. The black fur-blend angora jersey with long torso, dirndl skirt, leg-of-mutton sleeves and tied neck. *ROBERT YOUNG.*

well as sexy; and moderately priced as well as expensive.

Few hard and fast rules apply to the design of evening wear—that very special category of dress with which the designer gives free reign to whimsical fantasy, limited only by the practical considerations of size range and cost.

It is therefore not surprising to find quite contradictory opinions and statements made by various designers of evening wear, in addition to a tremendous range of styling. The best advice that can be offered an aspiring designer is to look, study, and compare. Stay abreast of new fabric trends, and at all times be aware of your environment.

DESIGNERS' COMMENTS

Paris designer Tan Guidicelli wants a woman in evening clothes ". . . to look like she's an object for a man. I think of my evening dresses in a Delilah way—very seductive."*

* *WWD*, 12/4/75, p. 1.

Black jersey crepe evening dress with beige chenille trim. Inspired by Roman costume (Tan Guidicelli). *ROBERT YOUNG.*

New York designer Halston likes ". . . complicated cuts and swirled-seamed things."*

SOURCES OF INSPIRATION

Sources of inspiration are environmental as well as ethnic and historical. Hand-painted and air-brushed floral and geometric prints on silk, chiffon, and other fabrics are decorating evening wear.

* *WWD*, 12/31/75, p. 3.

Lettuce-edged gray chiffon tunic with hand-painted roses over matching gray Nyesta pants (Susan Kyle, New York). *ROBERT YOUNG.*

89

White corded silk halter gown with airbrushed red, blue, and black circles (Fabrice Simon, New York).

New York designer Halston likes complicated cuts and swirled-seamed lines. Design on right, is a creampuff-shaped top over slim pants, in lavender and mauve ombré silk. *KENNETH PAUL BLOCK.*

90

St. Laurent's dotted tunic with wide deep side slits and hip sash; the rose-printed
tunic over a narrow black skirt banded in red at the hem. *KENNETH PAUL BLOCK.*

Italian designer Valentino's 1976 collection featured Moroccan, Tunisian, and Syrian inspired prints and silhouettes. Valentino studied the mosques and dwellings of these countries and borrowed the details to put on his fabrics.

Yves St. Laurent's tunics are Orient inspired. Soft and silky fabrics in vivid reds, jades, violets, oranges, and fuchsias express his exotic outlook toward color for evening.

EXERCISE 35

Go to the library and take along some pencils and tracing paper. Spend some time researching the folk and historic costume collections.

Sketch or trace those costumes or details of costumes which may be adapted for your own designing purposes. Whenever you find an interesting or unusual pattern construction, draw it with special attention to the seaming. Label each sketch with its historic period and/or place of origin.

Do not limit yourself to apparel. Shoes, hats, bags, belts, jewelry, and textiles are also excellent sources of inspiration.

Start a scrapbook with these sketches. Add to it whenever possible.

notes

CHAPTER TWENTY
illustrating jersey

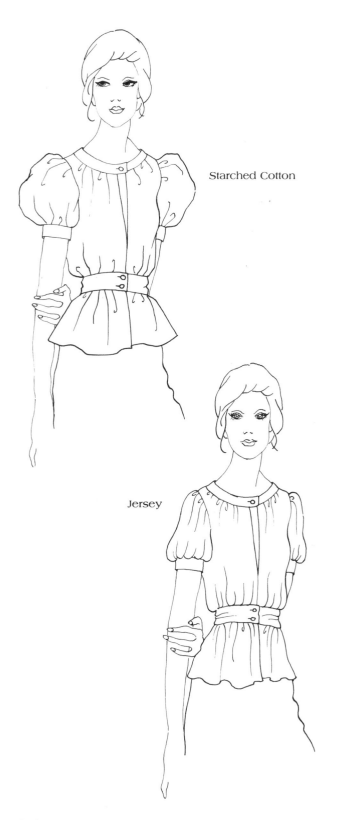

Starched Cotton

Jersey

Jersey is a knit fabric made of wool, cotton, or synthetic fibers. Very soft, lightweight, and stretchable, it is perfect for shirring and draping, falling in gentle folds or hugging the figure when bias-cut.

It has a range of surface finishes from shiny to matte; can be printed or plain; and is often crushproof and drip-dry as well.

Its ultra feminine qualities reveal the structure of the body as the fabric clings and flows gently with every movement. For all these reasons, jersey is ideally suited to the design of a variety of women's clothing, including travel, vacation, and evening wear.

PROCEDURE

When illustrating jersey, accentuate its softness and drapeable qualities. Stiffer fabrics stand away from the body and folds are crisp, whereas jersey hugs the body, stretches with its movements, and falls in fluid folds.

The pattern for the starched and jersey blouses illustrated is the same—the difference is in the drawing of the fabric.

EXERCISE 36

On tracing paper over a thumbnail croqui, design five jersey evening outfits particularly suitable for vacation travel. Refer to your costume scrapbook (discussed in *Chapter 19, Exercise 35*) as a source of inspiration for some of the designs.

Select one for illustration. Transfer it (full size) to a sheet of water color paper. Using values of gray, paint it with a partial wash and finish with an accented brush line.

London designer Janice Wainright likes her evening jerseys soft and clinging, with classic bias and spiral cuts.

Her novel use of trimming details include floral embroidery. *STEVEN MEISEL.*

CHAPTER TWENTY-ONE

illustrating satin

Satin is a smooth, lustrous fabric with a glossy surface and dull back. Made either from silk, man-made fibers or combinations of these yarns, it usually has a good firm body and holds its shape well. Glossiness and firmness of body are the two main visual attributes of satin illustrations.

PROCEDURE

STEP 1. Set up your supplies: a finished drawing on water color paper mounted on a drawing board; two containers of clean water; blotters; brushes; paints; palette; four washes of the color of your choice for the accented brush lines.

> Wash #1—light
> Wash #2—medium
> Wash #3—medium-dark
> Wash #4—dark

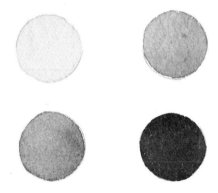

STEP 2. Since satin must be rendered on a wet ground which tends to dry quickly, it is best to paint the garment in sections, one at a time, and to let each section dry before proceeding to the next. Select the section to be painted first, and brush it with clean water.

STEP 3. While the section you have covered with water is still damp, brush in some of the lightest wash (wash #1). Use either a number 3 or 4, medium-sized brush. Only a small amount of paint is required, as it will spread out when it makes contact with the wet paper.

The paint is applied only where shadows fall. As satin is shiny, areas with highlights are left completely free of color, showing up as pure white in the finished painting.

STEP 4. While wash #1 is still damp, use a small amount of wash #2 to build a second shadow. The edges of wash #2 should blend slightly into the first wash.

If there is too much blending, so that no distinction can be made between each wash, then wash #1 was too wet when wash #2 was applied.

STEP 5. Change to a smaller brush. Build another layer of shadow with wash #3 while the previous application of paint is still slightly damp.

Permit the painted section of the garment (in this illustration a sleeve) to dry thoroughly before moving on to another area, otherwise "running" will occur.

STEP 6. Move on to another section of the garment and paint it in the same way.

Do not forget to brush on a layer of clear water before applying the next three washes.

STEP 7. When the entire costume is painted and thoroughly dry, finish with accented brush lines, using the darkest of the four washes (wash #4).

Sleeve is brushed with water.   Step 2

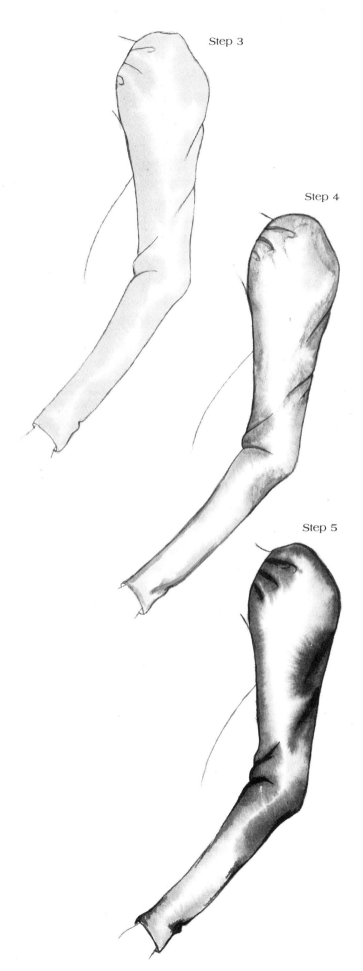

Step 3

Step 4

Step 5

Step 6

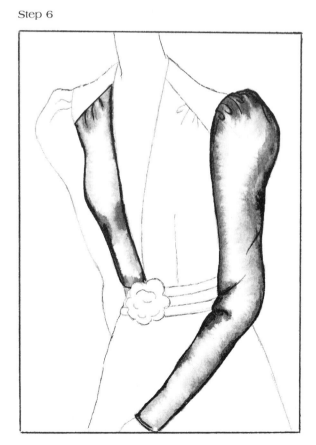

97

Finished painting with accented brush lines. Each section is painted separately. Skirt is painted in two sections divided by a center seam. Shadows fall behind folds; highlights are left unpainted.

EXERCISE 37

On tracing paper over a thumbnail croqui, design five satin evening outfits.

Use trimming on some of the designs (appliqué, fabric flowers, embroidery, braid, beading, frogs, clasps, belts, buckles, piping, banding, etc.).

Select one for illustration and transfer it (full size) to a sheet of water color paper. Follow the painting procedure outlined in Steps 1 through 7.

notes

illustrating velvet

Velvet was originally made of silk but is now more often constructed of synthetic fibers. It has a smooth, soft, luxurious pile surface which varies in texture and appearance from one type of velvet to another; just as its weight and thickness also vary.

Nevertheless, the following procedure satisfactorily applies to the painting of most velvet fabrics. There are a few small drawbacks to the method:

1. Only certain colors are illustrated effectively—all dark colors except black;

2. It is a somewhat lengthy and time-consuming process.

But for the lack of a faster, more effective technique which yields equally attractive results, this one will suffice.

PROCEDURE

STEP 1. Set up your work space. In addition to the usual supplies, add a box of cotton-tipped swabs (Q-Tips, etc.) and a tube of water color paint of any dark color except black.

STEP 2. Squeeze some paint out of the tube and dilute it to a thick and creamy consistency.

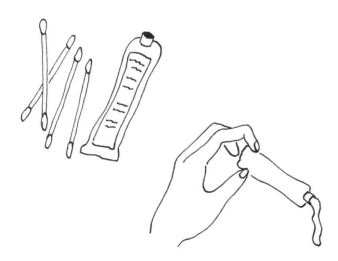

STEP 3. Cover the entire garment with the mixture, except for very thin lines to be left unpainted wherever there are seams, darts, the edges of folds, and the edges of overlapping collars or cuffs.

Use a large brush for the larger areas, and a fine brush when painting around seams, darts, etc.

STEP 4. When the first coat of paint is dry (after about ten minutes) repeat the process a second time.

There will now be two applications of paint instead of one, with the same fine, unpainted lines showing through.

STEP 5. While the second coat of paint is still wet use a cotton swab to "pull out" some color from areas of the garment which would normally be highlighted.

This is achieved by rubbing the swab over a painted area so that some of the paint comes off on the tip. Do not rub all the way through to the white paper. Remove just enough paint to lighten the section you want highlighted.

NOTE: Shadows fall under the bust —highlights are on top of the bust. Shadows fall behind folds—highlights are on the roll of the fold.

STEP 6. Slightly dampen a number 2 brush and run it lightly across all the unpainted lines, pulling a small amount of color into them.

EXERCISE 38

On tracing paper over a thumbnail croqui, design five velvet evening outfits. Include a few two-piece pantsuits.

Use 15th, 16th, or 17th century European costume as a source of inspiration for some of the designs. Sketch the original costume as well as your adaptation.

Select one for illustration and transfer it (full size) to water color paper. Follow the painting procedure outlined in Steps 1 through 6.

EXPERIMENTAL PROJECT (OPTIONAL)

If you wish to experiment with pastel- or medium-toned velvet, try the following procedure:

STEP 1. Mix a thick and creamy wash by adding white paint to the color of your choice.

STEP 2. Cover the area to be painted with this wash. Let it dry for a few minutes.

STEP 3. With a clean brush dipped in clear water, wet the areas of highlight. Quickly apply a blotter to remove most of the paint on those areas.

STEP 4. Paint the remaining sections of the garment the same way. Let them dry thoroughly.

STEP 5. Pastel- and medium-toned velvets require shadows, which should be just slightly darker than the color of the velvet. Use a feathery dry-brush technique with crosshatch lines. (See Chapter 31, page 140 for a detailed description of dry-brush technique.)

STEP 6. Accented lines are applied only where touching up is essential, and in shaded areas.

CHAPTER TWENTY-THREE
illustrating chiffon

Chiffon is an ultra-thin transparent fabric made of cotton, silk, rayon, or synthetics; and is used primarily for evening wear, cocktail dresses, dressy blouses, and elegant lingerie.

Some chiffon fabrics have more body than others, and these are illustrated in the same way as sheers (see Chapter 17). Silk and rayon chiffon, however, are so delicately soft and filmy that a somewhat different technique is required for their illustration, but only when

a great deal of fabric is used, as is the case with gathers or many flares.

PROCEDURE

STEP 1. Develop a finished pencil drawing on water color paper showing the skin and hinting at the undergarment as well as the transparent overgarment.

On a drawing, gathers and flares

Pencil drawing showing skin and undergarment painted with a flat wash and built-up shadows. Steps 1 and 2

Chiffon is painted over skin and undergarment. Darker areas represent folds in the fabric. Steps 3 and 4

are indicated by very fine pencil lines which create the illusion of chiffon. In order to avoid having these lines smear when later painted over, draw them with a very hard lead (4H or 6H); or just leave them out until they can be inserted with paint instead of pencil.

STEP 2. Paint the undergarment and/or skin with a flat wash and built-up shadows.

Let the painting dry for about an hour before continuing. It needs to "set" firmly so that there will be no smearing or blending when the chiffon is painted over it.

STEP 3. Mix a wash for the first layer of chiffon. Brush it over the entire chiffon garment, covering the undergarment and skin. Let it dry thoroughly before continuing.

STEP 4. Mix a slightly darker wash of the same color. Wherever there are folds in the fabric, add another layer of wash.

STEP 5. When thoroughly dry, mix a slightly darker wash for a second layer of folds.

Wherever there are folds in the fabric which overlap each other, paint them with this darker wash.

STEP 6. Let the previous application of paint dry thoroughly. Using a number 1 or 2 brush, paint a lot of very fine lines wherever the chiffon is gathered or falls in many folds, in the

A second layer of folds shows overlapping layers of chiffon. Step 5

Finished painting with accented brush lines. Steps 6 and 7

same way you would draw these lines if using pencil.

STEP 7. Mix another wash, slightly darker than the previous one, for the finishing touches and accented brush lines.

With it outline the hemline, bottom edges of sleeves, etc., or wherever a rolled hem is found on the garment. Also accent seams and darts.

Notice the shape of the lines wherever there is a rolled hemline.

EXERCISE 39

On tracing paper over a thumbnail croqui, design five chiffon evening gowns. Include some gathers, flares, or bias drapes.

Refer to Egyptian, Greek, or Roman costume as a source of inspiration for at least one sketch. Draw the original costume as well as your adaptation.

Select one design for illustration and transfer it (full size) to water color paper.

Follow the painting procedure outlined in Steps 1 through 7.

EXPERIMENTAL PROJECT (OPTIONAL)

To paint white chiffon, try the following procedure:

White chiffon should not be rendered on a white background, so substitute either of the following for water color paper:

1. A heavy quality gray, tan, or pastel colored charcoal paper, which may be purchased by the sheet;

2. A pastel colored illustration board— heavier than charcoal paper, but will not buckle with the application of water.

STEP 1. Develop a finished pencil drawing with a very hard lead (4H or 6H) so that it does not smear when painted over.

STEP 2. Mix two washes for the skin and undergarment. Add white paint to each so that they become more opaque than transparent. The background color of the paper should not show through the skin or undergarment.

STEP 3. Paint them with a flat wash and built-up shadows. Let the paper or the illustration board dry thoroughly before continuing.

STEP 4. Use white paint thinned with water for a transparent chiffon wash. Test the transparency of the wash. If too opaque, add more water.

STEP 5. Brush the wash over the entire chiffon garment, covering the skin and undergarment with it. Let it dry thoroughly before continuing.

STEP 6. To paint the folds, add more white to the chiffon wash. Folds should be whiter than the rest of the fabric.

STEP 7. To paint a second layer of folds, add even more white to the previous wash.

Areas which have many folds should be whiter and therefore less transparent than the rest of the garment, but only on the folds.

STEP 8. Fine lines, edges of rolled hems, accented brush lines on seams, darts, etc., are rendered with a creamy, very white, undiluted paint.

notes

CHAPTER TWENTY-FOUR
sequins and lamé

Sequins are small, shiny disks of metal or plastic which are pierced and sewn onto garments in decorative patterns, or they may also cover the entire fabric. Lamé is a shiny textile made with metallic yarns. Both are used primarily in the design of evening wear and accessories. Their methods of illustration are roughly similar with a few minor differences.

ILLUSTRATING SEQUINS—PROCEDURE

STEP 1. Paint the garment with a flat wash and built-up shadows. A medium to dark color is more effective when illustrating sequins. Include the accented brush lines.

STEP 2. Mix a thick and creamy batch of

Start with a flat wash and built-up shadows. Include the accented brush lines.

Step 3

wash by adding white paint to the color used for the garment. This mixture should be considerably lighter than the painted garment.

STEP 3. Wherever there are highlights on the garment, paint a series of random dots with the light colored paint mixture.

Let the paint dry thoroughly before continuing.

STEP 4. Squeeze a small amount of white paint onto your palette. If slightly watery, do not dilute it. The paint should be quite thick.

On top of the areas already painted

Step 4

with colored dots, add some white dots to accentuate the highlights.

ILLUSTRATING LAMÉ—PROCEDURE

STEP 1. Paint the garment with a flat wash and built-up shadows. A medium to dark color is more effective when illustrating lamé. Include the accented brush lines.

STEP 2. When the painting is dry, wherever highlights should appear on the garment, work out a series of narrow, vertical pencil lines right on top of the paint.

STEP 3. Squeeze some white paint onto your palette. Keep it thick.

With a number 0 or 1 brush, paint a series of very tiny white dots along the vertical pencil lines.

EXERCISE 40

On tracing paper over a thumbnail croqui, design five evening outfits either decorated with sequins or made of lamé.

Select one for illustration and transfer it (full size) to water color paper. Follow the outlined painting procedure for sequins or lamé.

EXPERIMENTAL PROJECTS (OPTIONAL)

PROJECT 1: GOLD AND SILVER LAMÉ—If you wish to experiment with gold or silver lamé or sequins, use water soluble metallic gold or silver paint. If water soluble paint is not available and you purchase turpentine soluble paint, use a special brush set aside for this purpose and clean it as quickly as possible after use.

SEQUINS 1. Build shadows directly on the white paper using values of yellow to light brown water color paint for gold sequins; values of gray for silver sequins.

2. Include the accented brush lines (light brown for gold sequins; gray for silver sequins).

3. Paint circular dots with the

107

Steps 1 and 2 Illustrating lamé

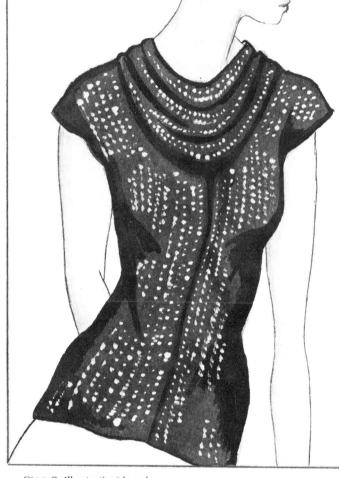

Step 3 Illustrating lamé

metallic paint wherever high-lights fall. In areas of shadow, sequins can be illustrated as a few circular lines rather than solid circles.

LAMÉ **1.** Cover the entire garment with a flat wash of the gold or silver paint. When thoroughly dry, apply a second layer of paint.

2. Leave the garment unshaded. Use brown paint for the accented brush lines on gold lamé; and dark gray for silver.

PROJECT 2: INDIA INK ILLUSTRATION—For an india ink illustration of lamé, use the following procedure:

1. Do a line drawing of the garment.

2. Wherever there are shadows, indicate them with black dots. Keep them sparcely scattered in light shadow areas; and thickly concentrated in dark shadow areas.

3. Add little sparkle lines to exaggerate the effect.

108

Illustrating lamé using india ink.

109

notes

UNIT 9
sleepwear and loungewear

CHAPTER TWENTY-FIVE
sleepwear

The calf-length sleep dress is of polyester crepe with a delicate floral print (Farr-West, California). *GLEN TUNSTULL.*

"Sleepwear" is a department-store term which conveniently lumps together a number of separate items that are sold in the same place. These include pajamas, nightgowns, ensembles, and robes.

PAJAMAS AND GOWNS

This category of sleepwear offers the imaginative designer a great deal of creative leeway. Styling can be seasonal, and varies from sweet to sexy to strictly tailored.

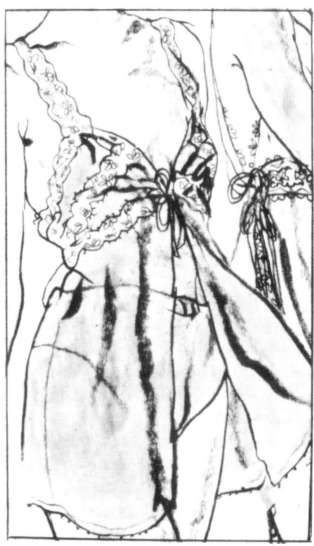

A sensuous baby doll in Anti-Cling Crepeset® (Van Raalte).

FABRICS—Fabrics are also diverse, ranging from delicate sheers to bulky sweatshirt knits. Particularly popular are brushed nylons and stretch terry cloth (for winter), tricot knits, polyester gauze, and permanent press cottons; plus a host of synthetic and natural fiber combinations, either solid colored or with floral prints.

POPULAR DESIGN ELEMENTS—Sleepwear designers make particular use of ruffles, flounces, elasticized shirring, smocking, tucking, piping, banding, drawstrings, and spaghetti bows and straps. Commonly employed trimmings are eyelet, lace, pleated and gathered ruching, embroidery, and ribbon.

FACTORS TO CONSIDER—The main factors to consider in the design of pajamas and nightgowns are comfort and easy care. These factors do not restrict the creation of ultra-feminine or lavishly trimmed sleepwear—they are simply built into the design.

For example, fabrics are usually drip-dry or permanent press, minimizing the amount of time required for their care. Sleeping comfort requires room for movement, so silhouettes are generally limited to the shift, tent, baby doll, empire, and an occasional A-line.

In addition to providing freedom of movement, these silhouettes (especially when designed with low-cut necklines) can be pulled over the head, eliminating the bulk, discomfort, time, and expense of plackets, buttons, and zippers.

ROBES

Although purchased in the sleepwear section of department stores, robes are not designed for sleeping. They function as cover-ups; to be worn alone or with something else underneath. Robes are also used for lounging, and as such they overlap the "Loungewear" category of feminine apparel (see Chapter 28).

Seasonal changes affect styling and choice of fabric. Fleece, velour, and quilting are winter favorites, while terry cloth is a year-round seller. Spring into summer lines are usually lightweight, drip-dry, and pastel colored or gayly printed.

There are "dressy" robes and casual

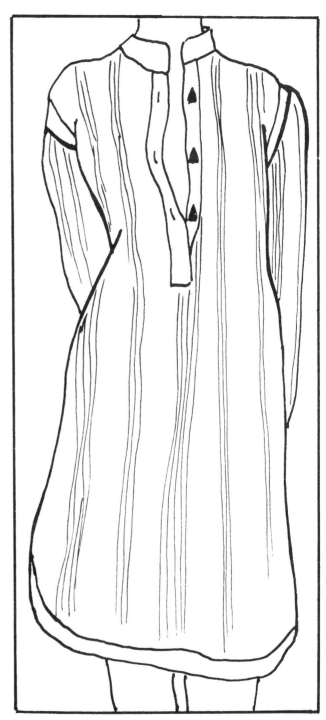

Men's wear inspired nightshirt in striped polyester and cotton (Rudi Gernreich for Lily of France).

robes; robes for entertaining and robes for cleaning house; robes for keeping warm and robes for staying cool; robes which can answer the doorbell and those which never leave the bedroom.

FACTORS TO CONSIDER—Factors to consider

113

Left: Empire silhouette nightgown with embroidered straps, gathered ruffles, tucks, piping, and a spaghetti bow (Kayser). Right: Smock silhouette with lace yoke and sleeve insets (Audra Arnsdorff for Lady Weldon).

in the design of robes fall primarily in the area of construction:

1. Robes which can be donned quickly and simply are preferred to those which require fussing. Wrap-arounds are especially practical, and front-zip closings are quick and easy. Front-button closings are acceptable, if the buttons are large enough. Avoid back closings and tiny buttons and buttonholes.

2. Robes should be roomy, providing freedom of movement and allowing for their function as cover-ups, so that pajamas or nightgowns may be worn underneath.

3. Loose sleeves and dropped armholes are favored over closely fitted ones. Bracelet length sleeves fit the long arm and the short, whereas full-length sleeves may require alteration. Practical winter robe sleeves have wide facings. This type of sleeve can be worn full-length (for warmth) or rolled back to create a shorter, cuffed sleeve which does not interfere with dining and other activities.

4. Pockets are a very desirable design feature.

5. Washable fabrics (and no-run colors) are more economical than those which require dry cleaning. Nylon quilting has an advantage over cotton, as it will not shrink and requires no ironing.

EXERCISE 41

Design five pairs of pajamas strictly for sleeping. Include some winter and summer; short and long. Name the fabric for each design.

Select one for illustration and transfer it to water color paper. Paint it with any technique of your own choosing.

EXERCISE 42

Design five summer robes. Include some casual robes which could function in the kitchen as well as elsewhere, and a few more elegant styles with at least one print.

Select one for illustration and paint it as you wish, attaching a swatch of fabric to the finished artwork.

White terry cloth with striped banding and oversized pockets (Clovis Ruffin).

Three elegant robes designed for the holiday season. Left: Montenapoleone's ruffled polyester georgette. Center: Bill Tice's obi-sashed polyester fleece. Right: Halston's V-necked velour caftan. *STEVEN STIPELMAN.*

116

notes

CHAPTER TWENTY-SIX
illustrating lace

There are something like ninety different types of lace, each of which can be produced in different patterns. To work directly from a swatch, therefore, seems the most sensible approach to illustrating lace. In lieu of that, however, the following procedure is a fast and simple method for effecting attractive results.

Step 1

Step 2

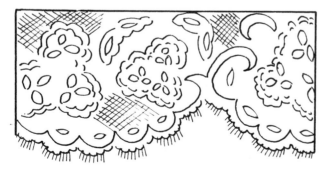

Step 3

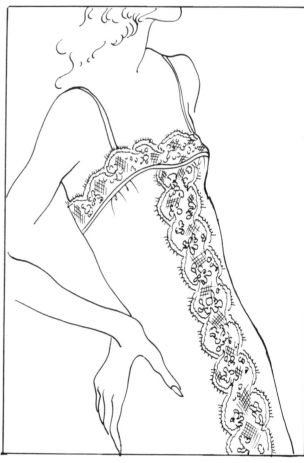

Lace Trim: Show the border pattern on both edges, unless one edge is sewn into a seam.

PROCEDURE

STEP 1. Work out a lace pattern with a border design.

STEP 2. Insert some crosshatch lines between the pattern to indicate a backing.

STEP 3. Add a series of small lines extending up from the edge of the border.

EXERCISE 43

On tracing paper over a thumbnail croqui, design five nightgowns or nightgown-robe ensembles which utilize some lace.

Select one for illustration and transfer it (full size) to water color paper.

Paint it with a partial wash in values of gray. Use a fine brush and black paint to render the lace.

EXPERIMENTAL PROJECTS (OPTIONAL)

If color is preferred, then:

1. Experiment with colored lace painted over pale skin tones, and with water color paint mixed with Chinese White or tempera for pastel and opaque effects.

2. Use gray or brown charcoal paper as a background instead of water color paper. Illustrate the lace with white paint or other colors mixed with it.

3. Use more than one color; try a multi-colored lace pattern.

Lace by the Yard: Show a border pattern only where the edge of the fabric is exposed (at the neckline, hem, etc.).

CHAPTER TWENTY-SEVEN
illustrating quilting

Quilting is a technique of joining together two layers of fabric with a lightweight filling in between by top stitching with criss-crossed lines in diamond or other patterns. Because of the additional warmth provided by its layering, quilting is ideal for winter robes.

PROCEDURE

STEP 1. Draw the garment.

STEP 2. Insert the criss-crossed lines at diagonals to the straight grain of the fabric.

STEP 3. At the edges of the garment, connect the diagonals with slightly curved lines.

STEP 4. For added effect, use broken lines to simulate stitching.

Step 1

Step 2

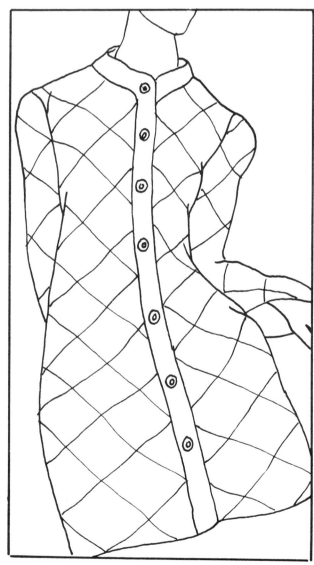

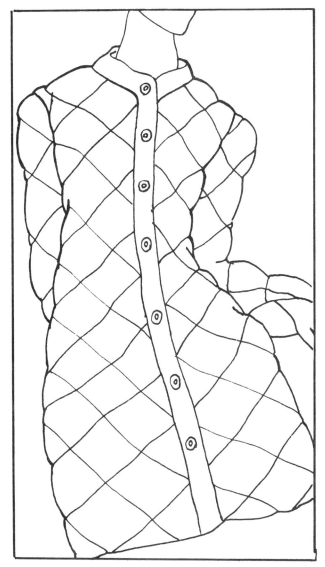

Step 3

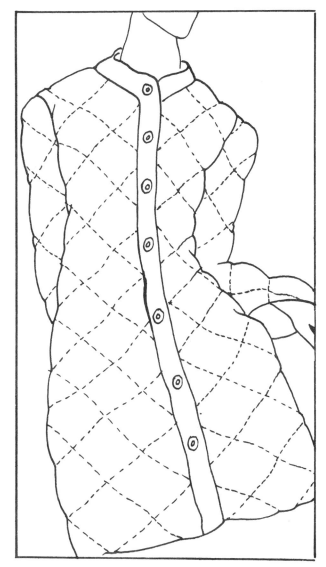

Step 4

EXERCISE 44

On tracing paper over a thumbnail croqui, design five winter robes, some of which are quilted.

Concentrate on design details such as closings, collars, and pockets. Take advantage of the possibilities of trimming (frogs, braid, fringe, appliqué, embroidery, etc.).

Use an Asian costume as a source of inspiration for at least one robe. Sketch the original costume as well as your adaptation.

Select one for illustration and transfer it (full size) to water color paper. Paint it in color with a flat wash and built-up shadows.

121

CHAPTER TWENTY·EIGHT
loungewear

For busy homemakers and mothers—The ultra practical approach to loungewear design. The ''lounge dress''—Inside pockets, top-stitched yoke, rolled sleeves, zippered front and rope belt in polyester and cotton chintz (Delores Loyola for Splendor-Lee). *CATHERINE CLAYTON.*

Loungewear is a category of feminine apparel which in recent years has demonstrated a booming growth rate; in popularity, sales, and the number of designers creating special loungewear collections.

This trend seems to be related to the American life style—an affluent society, leisure time, a variety of home-centered activities, and a growing body of career women wanting and willing to pay for clothes that fill the gap between work and sleep.

TYPES OF LOUNGEWEAR

While designed primarily for at-home wear, some of it does, in fact, "step out," as there are numerous approaches to loungewear design. It can vary from very intimate (resembling sleepwear) to very casual (resembling sportswear) to very elegant (resembling evening wear).

SPECIAL FEATURES—But loungewear that withstands the test of time will have certain salient features. These are comfort, attractiveness, ease-of-care, and flexibility (a flexibility which permits movement from living room to kitchen; from privacy to company).

POPULAR LOOKS—Pajamas, pants, tunics over pants, jumpsuits, T-shirts, caftans, smocks, and long and short sun dresses are especially popular loungewear looks, while fabrics are even more diverse.

EXERCISE 45

On tracing paper over a thumbnail croqui, design five pieces of loungewear. Work from fabric swatches.

Select one for illustration. Transfer it (full size) to water color paper.

Paint it in color with a flat wash and built-up shadows; or with a wet-wash technique if a print.

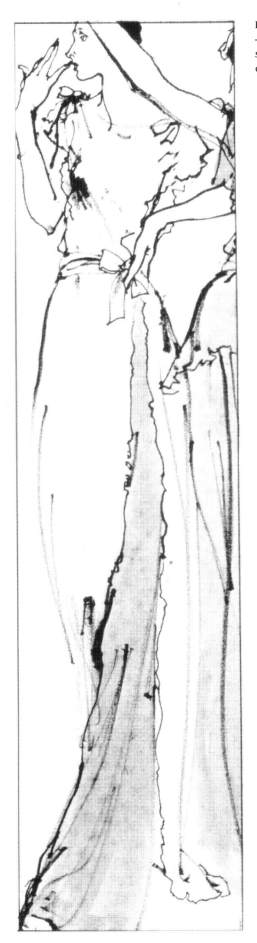

Fernando Sanchez' formal loungewear
—The long silver-gray tunic over·
spice-colored pants, in silk crepe de
chine. *KENNETH PAUL BLOCK.*

Enkalure® nylon pajama set features kimono sleeves,
pearl buttons, and a spaghetti sash (Pearl, Private Treas-
ures). *DOROTHY LOVERRO.*

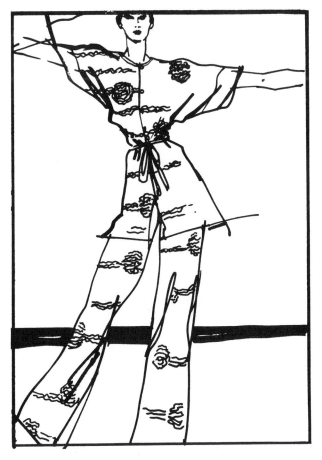

123

notes

UNIT 10 outerwear

CHAPTER 31—ILLUSTRATING FUR

THE DRY-BRUSH TECHNIQUE

PERSIAN LAMB

BROADTAIL

LEOPARD

BEAVER

SEAL

MINK

SABLE

ERMINE

FOX

   Red Fox

   Black Fox

RACCOON

EXERCISE 49

CHAPTER 32—SUITS

STYLING AND CONSTRUCTION

EXERCISE 50

CHAPTER 33—LEATHER AND SUEDE

ILLUSTRATING LEATHER—PROCEDURE

ILLUSTRATING SUEDE—PROCEDURE

EXERCISE 51

notes

CHAPTER TWENTY-NINE

coats

The coat designer requires some basic knowledge of tailoring techniques, which differ from the techniques applied in dressmaking. These differences result primarily from the function of coats, their consequent construction, and the use of heavier coating fabrics.

As the very last garment to be donned before stepping out, a coat functions as a cover-up to several layers of clothing worn underneath. It is therefore constructed to provide ample room for movement and layering. Coats are also built for warmth. Suits, separates and bulky knitwear have almost entirely replaced them in popularity as outerwear for spring and fall, so that the majority of coats are designed for winter. Strictly seasonal lines, however, are distinguished by differences in color, weight, and styling.

CONSTRUCTION

The application of tailoring techniques to the construction of coats involves the use of facing, interfacing, lining, interlining, and/or backing.

FACING—Facing is a sewing term used for self-fabric (same material as the garment) linings which are used only on certain parts of a coat—the collar, neckline, lapels, cuffs, hem; and on the inside of the coat closing—from the top of the neckline to the bottom of the hem. Occasionally, facing is made of fur or some other fabric, giving the impression that the entire garment is lined with it.

INTERFACING—Interfacing is a fabric inserted between the outside of a garment and its facing to give body and shape to the faced section. It is the stiffening agent in collars, lapels, cuffs, closings, etc. Traditional interfacings were canvas-like fabrics made of linen or linen and hair, unbleached muslin, or crinoline. These have been entirely replaced,

however, by a number of newer, nonwoven fabrics such as Pellon, Armo; and fusibles* such as Vilene and Solidot, among others.

LINING—Lining is found in all tailored coats except for an occasional summer coat; and fabrics vary with design and price range. Some linings such as crepe are very soft and pliable; others, like taffeta, are crisper. Pile, quilting, sheepskin and fur are bulky but warm.

INTERLINING—Traditional interlining is a loosely woven wool or cotton fabric inserted between a lining and the outer coat fabric to provide extra warmth. It may still be found in some custom-made or hand-tailored coats; but for the purposes of mass production, this type of interlining has been replaced by fusible interlinings which are fused directly to the back of the coating.

Fusibles can be used with practically every type of fabric, as well as leather and fur. Depending on the type employed, any amount of body, support, crispness, flexibility, or rigidity can be given to a coating fabric, substantially widening its range of design possibilities.

BACKING—Traditional backing was a canvas-like fabric sewn directly to the back of a coating fabric to give it body and shape.

Fusibles and contemporary fabrics such as Pellon and Armo have gradually replaced the older canvas-like backings in the manufacture of ready-to-wear, as they are less expensive and easier to use. They are also versatile, functioning as backing, interlining, or interfac-

---

* Fusible fabrics are actually fused to other fabrics with the application of heat and pressure, either by hand irons or on pressing machines, and are unaffected by washing or dry-cleaning. They vary in weight, body, and stiffness; and are designed to be used with particular materials for specific purposes.

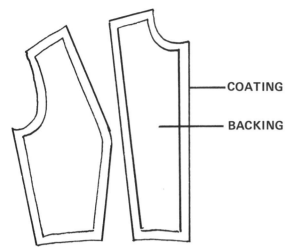

COATING

BACKING

Princess waist pattern showing backing attached to the back of its coating fabric.

B. If, however, darts are incorporated into a design, their excess pucker must be "shrunk in" with a steam iron; and the underlying layers of fabric should conform to the adjusted shape. Shrinking is easier to achieve with a loosely woven fabric such as basket weave, as opposed to a tightly woven fabric such as twill.

ing, depending on the type selected for use.

The entire front section of most mass-produced coats are completely backed from top to bottom with fusibles chosen for their particular weight and body. As pointed out above, backing may serve simultaneously as interlining, depending on its weight and body.

Budget-priced coats are often made with bonded coatings. Bonding is a process of joining together two fabrics by means of adhesive or foam. The coating shows on one side, and usually has a layer of acetate locknit or some other fabric bonded to its back, providing built-in body. The disadvantage of bonded coatings is that they are not selective—sleeves will be backed as well as the rest of a coat, and the finely tailored detailing made possible by softer fabrics may have to be bypassed.

CONSTRUCTION AND FABRIC AFFECT DESIGN

Basic coat construction involving the use of tailoring techniques, and the potentials and limitations of coating fabrics strongly influence the design of coats. These factors affect design in numerous ways, some of which are discussed below:

1. Where shaping is desired, tailored coats are usually constructed with seams rather than darts. There are a number of reasons for this preference:
   A. Seams do not "pucker" as do darts. A smoother fit is achieved through seaming.

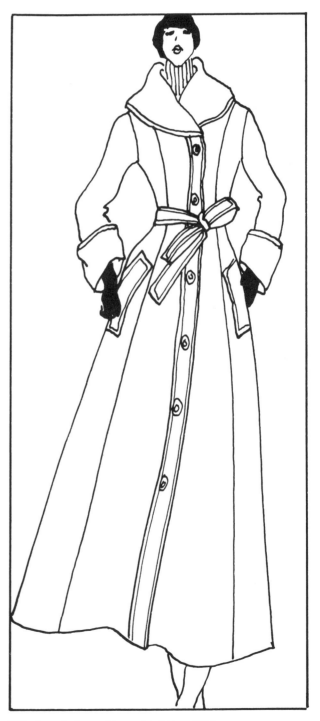

Fitted coat shaped by princess seams.

129

2. Bulky fabrics limit coat design to smart but simple lines. Details of construction are subordinated to silhouette because of the difficulties of "working" the fabric. In addition to their bulkiness, such fabrics are often loosely woven with a tendency to ravel, which is why excessive seaming and small pattern pieces are best avoided.

3. Thinner, lighter-weight fabrics lend themselves more readily to detailed design work, but require the use of backing or interfacing if shaping and body are desired.

4. The looser a coat, the more layers of fabric

Camel-colored cashmere, box-shaped coat requires little shaping (Jacques Tiffeau). *KENNETH PAUL BLOCK.*

The Dressmaker Coat

The "Perennial" Polo Coat

Chanel's '76 spring coat demonstrates a classic approach to coat design. Simply cut and novelty trimmed, fabric and silhouette are the major components. *KENNETH PAUL BLOCK.*

it can accommodate. Looser fitting coats take interlining better than snugly fitted ones.

STYLING

Despite the limitations of fabric and construction, coat styling is quite diverse. Between the opposite poles of tailored and dressmaker coats lies a range of styling which incorporates the best features of each. There are the classic and the trendy coats; the full and jacket lengths; minis, longuettes (midis), and maxis; daytime, evening, and sport coats; and the fur-trimmed or untrimmed styles.

THE DRESSMAKER COAT—Not subject to the same limitations as tailored coats. Made of lightweight spring into summer coating, they may or may not be lined; and have soft lines and intricate details more like those of a dress.

THE "PERENNIAL" POLO COAT—Double- or single-breasted, collared, buttonless, and tie-belted. It has been popular since the 1930's.

THE ENSEMBLE—Coat and dress are designed and coordinated to be worn together.

POPULAR DESIGN ELEMENTS

Fabric and silhouette are the outstanding features of coat design, but a number of other elements also play important roles. Collars and pockets, for example, are not only stylish but functional. Collars provide warmth as well as fashion (especially collars which can be worn up around the ears), while pockets are practically essential.

In addition to collars and pockets, seaming, stitching, buttonhole and button details, belts, buckles, and real or imitation fur trims are the most commonly applied motifs in coat design.

131

Fur Shawl Variation

Notched Shawl Variation

Spread Variation

Convertible Variation

COLLARS—There are no rules or regulations which determine the size or shape of a coat collar so long as it is comfortable, functional, and attractive. Some variations include: notched shawl, fur shawl, convertible, and spread (see illustrations).

POCKETS—Pockets are an expected feature of coat design. Although there are many types of pockets, certain styles are particularly adaptable for outerwear such as flap, slit, welt, hacking, cargo, patch, and seam pockets (see illustrations).

EXERCISE 46

Collect an ample supply of coating fabric swatches. Include solid colors, tweed, lightweight and winterweight fabrics.

For this exercise, select some solid-colored, lightweight samples. Set aside the tweed and winterweight fabrics for future exercises.

On tracing paper over a thumbnail croqui, design three spring coats and three ensembles. Ensembles may consist of matching coats and dresses, coats and skirts, coats and pants, or any other combination of garments

132

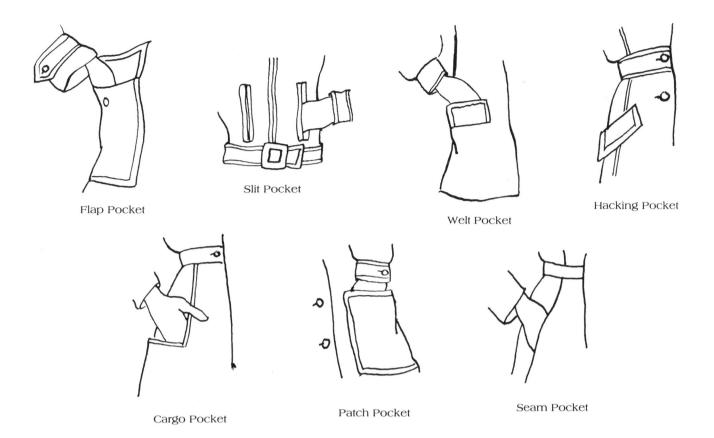

Flap Pocket

Slit Pocket

Welt Pocket

Hacking Pocket

Cargo Pocket

Patch Pocket

Seam Pocket

designed to wear as part of a coat outfit. Include some daytime designs and at least one for evening wear. Pay attention to details such as collars, pockets, closings.

Select one coat and one ensemble for illustration. Transfer the drawings (full size) to water color paper, and paint them in color with a partial wash.

The Ensemble—Matching striped wool coat and dress
(Marc Bohan for Christian Dior, Paris). *KENNETH PAUL BLOCK.*

134

notes

illustrating tweed

Procedure II

As their appearance varies tremendously with color, weave, and thickness and type of yarn, tweed is best illustrated directly from swatches of fabric. The following procedures, however, apply to the most popular types of tweed, and may therefore be used with or without sample fabrics.

SALT AND PEPPER AND NUBBY TWEED—THE "OVERALL" ILLUSTRATION: PROCEDURE I

STEP 1. Paint the background color of the garment with a flat wash.

STEP 2. Paint one layer of shadow only, considerably darker than the first wash. Use shadows sparingly, where really needed. Let the painting dry thoroughly.

STEP 3. Paint the accented brush lines.

STEP 4. With a number 0 or 1 brush, cover the garment with very fine dots that contrast with its background color. If you wish to experiment, use a "stipple" brush for the dots.

PROCEDURE II

STEP 1. Mix a medium to light wash. Give the garment a partial covering with this wash—treat it as if it were a shadow, falling where shadows fall.

STEP 2. Paint the accented brush lines.

STEP 3. Mix one or two darker washes and use them to cover the garment with fine dots.

HERRINGBONE TWEED— THE "OVERALL" ILLUSTRATION: PROCEDURE I

STEP 1. Paint the background color with a flat wash. Let it dry thoroughly.

Step 1

Step 2

Step 3

STEP 2. Using a hard pencil, work out a vertical line pattern on top of the flat wash. Follow the straight grain of the fabric.

STEP 3. Mix a wash for the tweed pattern, considerably darker than the background color. Paint a series of short, diagonal brush strokes along each vertical band.

Diagonal strokes on alternating bands move in the same direction, while strokes on the bands between move in the opposite direction.

This results in the brush strokes of adjacent bands coming together in a V-formation.

STEP 4. Shadows are applied after the herringbone pattern is painted.

Mix a wash for the shadow color—one or two values darker than the color of the first wash. Brush only one layer of shadow right on top of the tweed rendering. Use it very sparingly, where really needed.

Finish with accented lines.

PROCEDURE II

STEP 1. Mix a medium to light wash. Give the garment a partial covering with this wash—treat it as if it were a shadow, falling where shadows fall.

STEP 2. Mix a considerably darker wash for the herringbone pattern and cover the garment with it, following the straight grain of the fabric.

Finish with accented lines.

Procedure I, Step 4

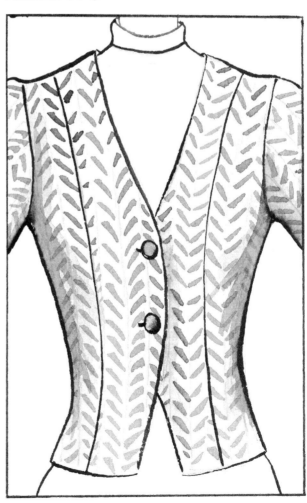

137

An alternative to the overall illustration is the partial illustration which is somewhat more casual, but highly effective and less time-consuming (upper left); or a flat illustration which does not follow the grainline of the fabric (center). *KENNETH PAUL BLOCK.*

THE "PARTIAL" TWEED ILLUSTRATION

An alternative to the "overall" illustration is the "partial" illustration which is somewhat more casual, but highly effective and less time-consuming; or a "flat" illustration which does not follow the grainline of the fabric (see illustrations on page 138).

There are a number of procedures for rendering a partial tweed. They apply to most tweed weaves, including salt and pepper, nubby, and herringbone.

PROCEDURE I

STEP 1. Paint the garment with a flat wash. Let it dry thoroughly.

STEP 2. Illustrate the tweed pattern directly on top of the flat wash. Treat the tweed as if it were a shadow, falling mainly on one side of the figure.

STEP 3. Finish with accented brush lines.

PROCEDURE II

STEP 1. Apply the tweed pattern directly to the white paper, in specific areas. Treat it as a shadow, falling mainly on one side of the figure.

STEP 2. With herringbone, accented lines on the garment should be either the same color as the tweed pattern, or black.

If salt and pepper, follow the usual accenting procedure.

If a nubby tweed with many colors, select the darkest color or black for accenting.

EXERCISE 47

Select a number of novelty weaves from among your sample swatches.

Practice painting these patterns on water color paper in two inch by two inch squares, until you have mastered the technique.

Select one and set it aside for *Exercise 48.*

EXERCISE 48

On tracing paper over a thumbnail croqui, design five short winter sport coats (hip to three-quarter length) for tweed fabrics including salt and pepper, herringbone, and at least one novelty weave.

Select three designs (one for each weave) for illustration, and transfer them (full size) to water color paper. Paint them in color with an "overall" or "partial" technique.

CHAPTER THIRTY-ONE
illustrating fur

THE DRY-BRUSH TECHNIQUE

One of the basic approaches to illustrating fur involves the use of "dry-brush," a painting technique which gives a soft, feathery appearance to the outline of a fur piece.

To apply the dry-brush technique:

1. Dip a brush into a wash.

2. Tap it against a blotter so that all excess paint is removed and the brush hairs separate.

3. Run the "dry" drush over the paper so that many fine hairlines are rendered simultaneously.

Some of the following procedures recommend the use of dry-brush, but a wet brush may be substituted, if preferred, by painting separate hairs with a number 0 or 1 brush.

PERSIAN LAMB

Persian Lamb is generally seen in black, brown, and gray. It is a short-haired, tightly curled fur with an intricate curlicue pattern.

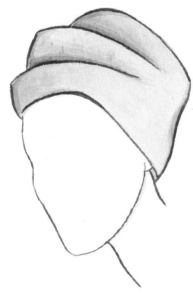

Persian Lamb: Step 1.

Persian Lamb: Step 2.

STEP 1. Apply a light-colored flat wash to the entire fur piece. Build shadows on this wash until the last shadow is very dark (for black Persian); or medium-dark (for brown and gray Persian).

STEP 2. When thoroughly dry, render the fur pattern with brush and water color paint, magic marker, or pen and ink. Accent the outer edges of the fur piece with slight curls to create the impression of a raised fur.

BROADTAIL

Broadtail is a flat, glossy fur with a delicate moiré pattern of wavy, primarily horizontal lines.

STEP 1. Paint the fur piece as you would black satin (see page 96)—but instead of starting with a clear water wash, start with a light gray wash. Brush in successive layers of shadow while previous ones are

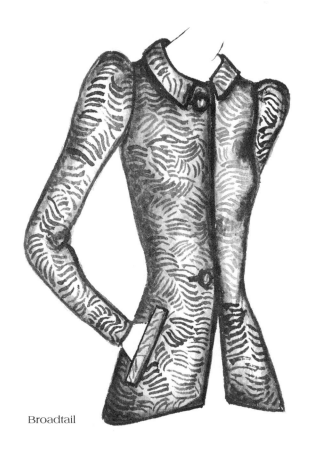

Broadtail

Leopard

still damp, until the last shadow is black.

STEP 2.	When the paper is almost dry, brush in the broadtail pattern with a dark gray-black color. Use wavy lines moving mostly in a horizontal direction; but vary their tilt or angle, shape, and size.

STEP 3.	When thoroughly dry, finish with black accented lines which show occasional breaks, indicating the surface irregularity of the fur.

LEOPARD

Leopard is a smooth, very flat fur with an irregularly spotted pattern. Its background is tawny (a dull yellowish color tinged with brown), and has an occasional darker streak in it indicating the backbone section of the skin. Markings are dark and take the form of spots and groupings resembling the paw prints of a cat.

STEP 1.	Work out the pattern in pencil.

STEP 2.	Cover the entire area to be painted with a dull, mustard-yellow wash.

STEP 3.	Shadows are brushed in while the first wash is slightly damp. Start with a medium brown mixed with a touch of black, and progress to a dark brown also mixed with a touch of black. Shadows will get lighter as they dry.

STEP 4.	When thoroughly dry, paint the pattern with a very dark wash mixed from black and brown. Use a medium brown for the accented lines.

BEAVER

Beaver is a luxurious, velvety-brown fur with a gray-blue cast. Illustration requires practice and experimentation for total mastery. The same painting procedure may be used for *mouton, nutria,* and *otter.*

STEP 1.	Mix three washes:

#1—A very pale brownish-gray;

#2—A rich creamy brown with some black added to it;

#3—A dark black wash with a touch of brown (for shadows and accenting).

141

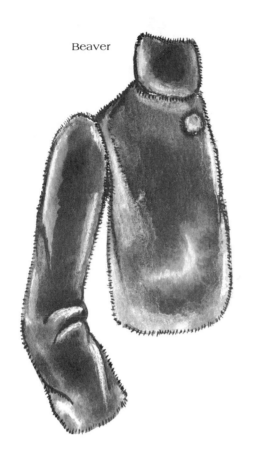

Beaver

Seal

STEP 2. Complete one section at a time (a collar, sleeve, etc.). Cover the area to be painted with wash #1.

STEP 3. While the section is still damp but not wet, cover it with wash #2 except for areas of highlight. Highlights appear especially on the edges of the garment.

STEP 4. If the paint spreads and blurs too much, quickly remove the excess with the tip of a blotter where sharp highlights are required; and use a cotton-tipped swab to blot up larger areas.

STEP 5. This wash will fade while drying, so enrich it by adding more of the same color before the paper is completely dry. Make sure it does not run into areas of highlight, or they will need blotting up again.

STEP 6. When almost completely dry, use wash #3 to brush in an occasional shadow (around folds, buttons, etc.).

STEP 7. When completely dry, use a number 0 or 1 brush to accent the edges with very fine, short hairlines instead of the usual accented lines.

SEAL

Seal is a softer, more lustrous and flexible fur than beaver with lighter, sharper, and larger areas of highlight. The following procedure may be used for *imitation seal (sheared black-dyed mouton, Borgana,* etc.) as well as for *natural sealskin.*

STEP 1. Apply a clear water wash to the section to be painted. While still damp, brush in a very dark and creamy wash, leaving unpainted the areas of highlight. Use dark brown or black. Quickly remove any paint that runs into areas of highlight with the tip of a blotter.

STEP 2. When thoroughly dry, finish with accented brush lines, and if necessary, touch up highlights with white paint on a dry brush.

142

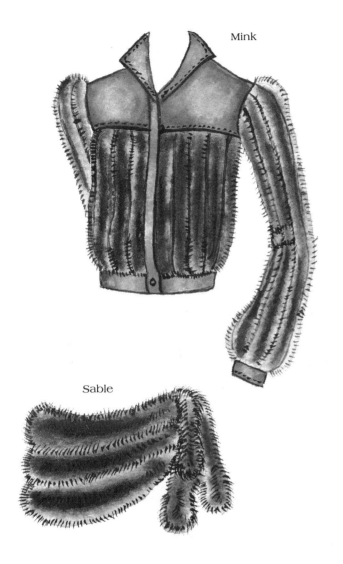

Mink

Sable

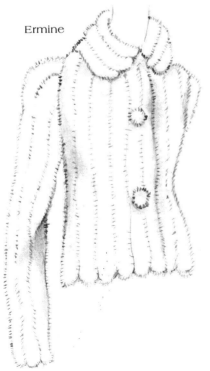

Ermine

MINK

Mink is a dense, soft fur with medium length hairs. Colors range from very dark brownish-black to white, with grays, blues, and beiges in between. Each pelt, whatever the color, has a darker streak running up its center.

STEP 1. Draw in the pelt pattern with pencil.

STEP 2. Cover the area to be painted with a flat wash very light to medium, depending on the color of the mink.

STEP 3. While still damp, paint an irregular streak up the center of each pelt. This color will fade while drying, so continue to darken it before it is completely dry.

STEP 4. When almost dry, separate each pelt with a very fine, irregularly accented line.

STEP 5. Paint the outer edges of the garment with very fine hairlines for a more detailed effect, or use a dry-brush technique with a number 2 or 3 brush.

STEP 6. For added detail, individual pelts may be separated by fine hairlines rendered with a wet or dry brush.

SABLE

Sable is a very expensive, luxurious fur with wider pelts and longer hairs than mink. Its preferred color is a very dark blue-black brown. *Follow the same procedure as for mink.*

ERMINE

Ermine comes from the same weasel family as mink. It is illustrated as white as possible.

STEP 1. Cover the section to be painted with clear water.

STEP 2. When the paper is slightly damp but not wet, build up some delicate shadows ranging from light to medium gray.

STEP 3. Paint the accented lines separating each pelt with light gray.

STEP 4. When thoroughly dry, finish the outside edges of the fur with very

Red Fox

Black Fox

Raccoon

fine hairlines. Use a dark gray wash for these lines, and for additional accenting if necessary. For added detail, individual pelts may also be separated by fine hairlines.

FOX

Fox is a dense, smooth long-haired fur with a wide pelt which comes in a number of colors including red, black, silver (black with silver tips), platinum, white, blue, and gray.

RED FOX

STEP 1. Apply a light wash.

STEP 2. While slightly damp but not wet, brush a medium orange-brown color down the center of the pelt. This shape should be irregular, wide to narrow, and mottled in effect.

STEP 3. When completely dry, brush in the long hairs with a dark orange-brown. Hair moves from the center out to the sides of the pelt.

STEP 4. Vary the color of the fur by brushing in some darker clusters of hair as well as some white ones.

BLACK FOX

STEP 1. Apply a medium-gray wash.

STEP 2. Paint a wide black shape down the center of the pelt while the paper is still wet, so that the paint blurs at the edges.

STEP 3. When absolutely dry (after at least a half hour), use black paint and a dry-brush technique to illustrate the fur, moving from the center out to the sides of the pelt.

STEP 4. When thoroughly dry, touch up the outer edges of the pelt with a wet number 0 or 1 brush.

RACCOON

Raccoon is similar to fox but has longer, coarser hairs. The color is mixed, with one pelt showing hairs of light golden-brown, medium gray-brown, rich dark brown, and platinum.

STEP 1. Cover the fur piece with a dull mustard-yellow wash.

STEP 2. While still damp, brush a dull medium gray-brown along the outside edges of each pelt, leaving a streak of the underlying wash showing down the center.

STEP 3. When thoroughly dry, use a dark gray-brown to brush in the long, coarse hairs moving from the center of the pelt out towards the edges.

STEP 4. Create a slightly mottled effect by brushing some black hairs over the brown ones in scattered areas.

EXERCISE 49

Select some winterweight wool swatches for this exercise.

On tracing paper over a thumbnail croqui, design three full-length evening winter coats with fur trim.

Transfer one design (full size) to water color paper. Practice painting the fur until you have mastered the technique; then complete the illustration.

CHAPTER THIRTY-TWO
suits

STYLING AND CONSTRUCTION

Suits, like coats, are designed primarily along seasonal lines. There are spring, summer, fall, and winter suits, all of which can be subdivided into a number of other categories such as dressmaker and tailored suits, walking suits, pantsuits, and so on.

Dressmaker suits (like dressmaker coats) have soft lines and fine details as contrasted with the sharply defined lines of tailor-made styles. They are worn from fall right through to spring, alone or beneath a coat; whereas tailored suits are more often designed as outerwear.

Tailored suits with a slightly military look in khaki wool gabardine with dropped drawstring waists (Marc Bohan for Christian Dior, Paris). *KENNETH PAUL BLOCK.*

Finely detailed Ultrasuede suit with subtle stitching and buttoned seam pockets at collar and hip (Michele Balice for Balice Fashions, New York). *STEVEN MEISEL.*

146

Three spring suits demonstrate mixed styling. Left: The strictly tailored, cream-colored polyester blazer with matching skirt and striped blouse (Mario Forte for Bona, New York). Center: The dressmaker look by Shannon Rodgers for Jerry Silverman (New York). Beige poplin cropped jacket over a black poplin skirt and floral-printed blouse. Right: The shirt-jacket rainsuit of bone polyester and cotton (Carol Anderson for Focus Sportswear, New York). *ROBERT YOUNG.*

147

Suits are lighter than coats and serve a different purpose. Consequently, certain features of coat construction (heavy coating fabric and interlining) are infrequently found in suits; while other features (lightweight fabric and very fine details) are often found in suits but rarely seen in coats. Naturally, the wealth of detailed styling in a suit or coat depends to a great extent upon the weight of its fabric, and that fabric's "workability."

Some suits (such as winter walking suits or winter pantsuits with long jackets) may have all the features of a short winter coat, including interlining. Other, mostly summer suits, might not be lined at all. Whether lined or unlined, all suits have facings, but interfacing is an optional feature. The more tailored a suit, the more likely it is to have interfacing, which gives body to the collar, lapels, closing, and cuffs.

EXERCISE 50

On tracing paper over a thumbnail croqui, design two summer, two fall, and two spring suits. Concentrate on the details of sleeves, collars, pockets, and closings.

Select two suits for illustration and transfer them (full size) to water color paper.

Paint them in values of gray and black, and finish with black accented brush lines.

notes

CHAPTER THIRTY-THREE
leather and suede

Leather is the prepared outside skin of an animal, which varies from very soft and smooth to very tough and grainy depending on the type of animal. *Suede* is the inside layer of skin which has been buffed to raise a slight nap. Both are used extensively for coats, jackets, skirts, vests, pants, suits and trimming.

Leather most often has a shiny surface whereas suede is always dull, which accounts for the different techniques of illustration.

ILLUSTRATING LEATHER—PROCEDURE

STEP 1. Mix a rich, creamy batch of wash with a medium to dark value.

STEP 2. Paint the garment in sections, one

Leather

Suits and coats of soft and supple cowhide (Luba, New York). *STEVEN STIPELMAN.*

at a time. Cover the first section to be painted with a clear water wash.

STEP 3. While the paper is still damp but not wet, brush the paint over it except for areas of highlight.

If the paint spreads into areas which should stay white, quickly apply the edge of a blotter to those areas, picking up the unwanted color. This layer of paint will get lighter as it drys.

STEP 4. When almost but not completely dry, use the same wash to brush in some shadows. This application of paint will appear darker than the first even though it is the same color.

STEP 5. When completely dry, finish with dark accented brush lines.

STEP 6. If necessary, certain areas may be touched up with white paint (folds on sleeves, for example) to accentuate the highlights.

ILLUSTRATING SUEDE—PROCEDURE

Paint the garment in sections, one section at a time.

STEP 1. Mix three batches of wash:

#1—A rich, creamy, light to medium color;

#2—A darker value of the same color;

#3—A very deep value for accented brush lines.

STEP 2. Paint a section with the lightest wash. While it is still wet, blot up areas of highlight with a cotton-tipped swab.

Do not *rub* the swab along the paper—this will merely smear the paint. Use a firm tapping motion with the tip, and change swabs as soon as each has lost its capacity to absorb more paint.

STEP 3. When the first layer of paint is almost dry, brush in some shadows with the second wash.

STEP 4. Blend the edges of the shadow

Suede

color into the first layer of paint with a clean, slightly moist brush.

STEP 5. When completely dry, finish with accented brush lines.

EXERCISE 51

On tracing paper over a thumbnail croqui, design five suits of leather or suede. Include some pantsuits.

Select one leather and one suede suit for illustration. Transfer them (full size) to water color paper. Follow the outlined painting procedures.

notes

UNIT 11
knitwear

CHAPTER THIRTY-FOUR
knitwear

The design of knitwear is a complex procedure requiring a good deal of technical knowledge. It is regretfully beyond the scope of this book to impart this knowledge to the aspiring designer, as knitwear design is a specialty deserving a separate course of study.

Nevertheless, a brief description of what is involved may hopefully encourage, rather than discourage, further investigation (a highly practical undertaking, for knitwear is a rapidly expanding industry in which the demand for designers and technicians frequently exceeds the supply).

THE KNITWEAR DESIGNER

The knitwear designer must first have a knowledge of dressmaking in order to design the various pieces of a pattern (collars, sleeves, waistlines, etc.).

Second, it is helpful to the designer to know something about knitting stitches and their measurements, in order to approximate the number of stitches to an inch. This is taken into consideration when designing the lengths and widths of the various pieces of a total pattern.

Third, she must understand the qualities of yarn—whether it stretches, whether it shrinks, how it hangs, its composition, and its wearability.

DESIGNING KNITWEAR

The process of designing knitwear will naturally vary from manufacturer to manufacturer, to a greater or lesser degree. For a medium-sized firm, however, a typical procedure goes something like this:

1. Designs are worked out first on paper. Sketches include style, type of stitch, color, and type of yarn.

2. The sketch then goes to a "set-up" man, who works on knitting machines or automatic looms, and makes the first patterns. He will confirm or deny the feasibility of producing a particular style with a particular stitch.

3. The design must also be approved by a coordinator or immediate supervisor, who considers such factors as style trends, production costs, distribution.

4. If all goes well, a sample garment is made up and adjusted to a sample size.

5. If the sample garment meets the required specifications for style, salability, etc., then a sample line is made up for that particular design. A sample line consists of one sample garment for each size, assuring perfect fit for the entire size range—for example: nine to fifteen, or eight to eighteen.

6. The actual production can take place anywhere in the world—either in a manufacturer's own factory, or in the factory of a subcontractor* who receives specifications on yarn, color, etc.

* A subcontractor is someone who is contracted by a manufacturer to do the actual construction of the manufacturer's designs. Subcontractors may produce for several or many manufacturers, making it a practical matter to operate a variety of highly technical and expensive machinery; whereas the small volume manufacturer cannot afford to do so. Subcontracting is an arrangement of convenience and value to both manufacturer and subcontractor. In addition, it is often done in countries where the cost of labor and materials is less expensive than in the manufacturer's own country, which further reduces his costs.

Long side-tied tabard (Trisha Sayad for Willis Avenue Bridge Works, New York).
ROBERT YOUNG.

155

CHAPTER THIRTY-FIVE
illustrating sweaters

Because of the tremendous diversity of knit and crochet stitches, patterns and designs, sweaters must be illustrated directly from original samples. The exception to this rule is knitwear which shows no special stitch or other pattern.

A strong difference between knitwear and other types of clothing is the way knit clothes hang on the body, clinging to and hugging it. Unless lined, knitwear tends to be very soft and supple, demanding its own particular illustrative techniques.

An exception to the rule of knitwear—No special stitch or other pattern.

Complex patterns must be illustrated from original samples. Left: The Icelandic wrap sweater (Reynolds). Right: The fluffy striped cardigan (Unger).
DOROTHY LOVERRO.

EXERCISE 52

Set aside one classroom session for sketching knitwear. Each student should wear his or her most unusual sweater to class that day.

Spend no more than five minutes on each rough sketch. Concentrate on important features only—the special stitching or novelty pattern. Note the colors.

Select two sketches and transfer them to water color paper over full-sized blouse croquis. Illustrate with paint.

If you wish to experiment, use a stiple brush for tweedy effects, and a dry-brush for a hairy (or cashmere) look.

NOVELTY KNITS

Cable Stitch

The Quilted Look

Jacquard prints and shag looping. Left: A navy, gray, and rust pull-on (Tami Sportswear). Right: The hand-knitted gray wool cardigan (Jantzen, Los Angeles). *ROBERT YOUNG.*

glossary

Acrylic—Fibers and yarns man-made from acrylic resins. Acrylics are easy to wash and quick-drying; wrinkle, moth and mildew resistant; have pleat retention.

Age Groupings—Garments grouped according to an age such as seven to ten years old.

Basket Weave—Variation of a plain weave, producing a checkerboard effect in one color.

Batiste—Fine soft lightweight cotton in plain weave, bleached or printed. Also made in sheer wool, sheer silk, and spun rayon.

Big Top—A full, loose, pull-over, hip-length blouse.

Bonding—Textile process involving the joining of two fabrics into one by means of adhesive or foam.

Borgana—Trademark of Borg Textiles for fake fur fabric resembling mouton lamb or sealskin.

Bracelet Length—Sleeve length ending slightly above the wrist.

Chroma—The purity of a color, or its freedom from white or gray.

Closing—The fastening together of two parts of a garment; or the devices used to close a garment.

Coating—Any fabric used for coats.

Complementary Colors—Colors found opposite each other on the color wheel. For example: red and green; orange and blue; and yellow and purple.

Contrast—The degree of difference between the values (amounts of light or dark) of adjacent colors.

Crinoline—An open weave, heavily sized cotton fabric used for stiffening, especially for interfacings.

Crochet—Method of making a garment, fabric, braid, or lace with yarn and the use of one hooked needle, done by hand or by machinery.

Croqui—Sketch of an undressed fashion figure with lines on it which correspond to the seams on a dressmaker's dummy. Used with an overlay of tracing paper for quick fashion drawings.

Crosshatch—A technique of shading with groups of lines applied in successive layers, each layer at right angles to the one beneath it.

Crush-proof—Wrinkle resistant when folded or packed for traveling.

Culottes—Women's pants of any length cut to look like a skirt; in other words, a divided skirt.

Décolleté—French adjective for a garment cut very low at the neckline.

Dotted Swiss—A crisp, sheer cotton decorated with evenly spaced dots of the same or a contrasting color, which are applied with adhesives, as in flock printing. The dots have a slightly raised, napped surface.

Dressmaker Coats and Suits—Not sharply tailored, with soft lines and intricate details more like those of a dress; may have a set-in belt and such details as tucks and pleats.

Drip-dry—Describing fabric that needs no pressing after washing.

Dry-brush—A technique of painting which gives a soft, feathery appearance to the area painted. Used frequently for illustrating fur, hair, and fuzzy yarns such as cashmere.

Easy-care Fabrics—Machine or hand washable, drip-dry, and crush-proof.

Facing—Sewing term for self-fabric lining used

158

on curved or irregularly shaped area of garment such as a neckline, lapels, collars, cuffs, or hem.

Fleece-backed fabric—Soft knit fabric with heavily napped surface on one side, used as linings in coats or for sweat shirts.

Flounce—A piece of gathered material used on a skirt, usually at the hem, singly or in a series.

Frog—An ornamental fastener made of braid or fabric cording, used for closing garments, especially some Chinese costumes.

Fusibles—Fabrics which are fused to other fabrics through the application of heat and pressure, either with hand irons or on pressing machines; and which withstand washing and dry-cleaning. Most fusibles are designed for use as interfacing, interling and/or backing; but there are many types of fusibles, each designed for a particular purpose or to be used with a specific material.

Gabardine—A durable, closely woven fabric with diagonal ridges, made of wool, rayon, cotton, and other fibers.

Glossy—Having a superficial luster, a sheen, polish, glaze.

Grainline—The direction of the straight grain, or warp (vertical) threads of a fabric.

Hard-edged—Having sharply defined outlines, not soft or blurry.

Intensity—Refers to the strength of a color, the degree of its pure pigment saturation.

Interfacing—Canvas of linen, linen and hair, unbleached muslin, crinoline, Pellon, Armo, etc., inserted between the outside and the facing of a tailored garment to give body and shape.

Interlining—Loosely woven woolen or cotton fabric used between the lining and outer fabric of a coat or jacket to provide added warmth and to retain shape.

Intimate Apparel—A department-store term for lingerie and underwear.

Jersey—Knitted fabric in plain stitch, made of wool, cotton, or man-made fibers, having a degree of stretchability.

Jodhpurs—Riding pants with drop-front or zipper closings that flare out at the thighs and have narrow straight-cut legs below the knee.

Khaki—A dull brownish-green wool or cotton fabric worn by the American, French and British forces during World War I and now adapted for contemporary fashion, especially sportswear.

Knickers—Knee-length pants cut full and held in just below the knee by straps or cuffs.

Knit Fabric—Made by interlacing loops of yarn or thread in various stitches and textures. Made by machine, allowing for a very wide variety of fabrics from very fine jerseys to bulky, imitation hand knits.

Kodel—Trademark of Eastman Kodak Company for various types of polyesters which are blended with other yarns to make durable-press fabrics.

Layering—A fashion trend which utilizes separate layers of garments worn on top of each other for added warmth. For example: pants and turtleneck sweater covered by a sleeveless tabard covered by a coat.

Lead Holder—A plastic or metal pen-shaped device into which a long piece of lead can be inserted and automatically fed out of a front opening. Leads are changeable, and only the tip of each lead requires sharpening as it wears down.

Leg-of-Mutton Sleeve—A woman's sleeve, wide and rounded at the shoulder, tapering to a snug fit on the lower arm, the shape of a leg of mutton. Variation may have shirring at the cap.

Light Box—A box frame with a light bulb and glass covering, used for tracing.

Line of Clothing—A category of garments which represent a manufacturer's production or presentation for a particular season. A manufacturer's summer sportswear line; a fall blouse line, etc.

Lining—Fabric, pile or fur used to finish the inside of a garment.

Longuette—Coats varying in length from mid-calf to a few inches above the ankle, introduced in 1970 in New York and Paris. Also used to describe skirt or dress length. Also called midi.

Lustrous—Having luster, shining, glossy.

Man-made Fibers—Fibers made totally by chemical means as well as fibers of regenerated cellulose.

Margin of Profit—The difference between the wholesale price of a garment and the cost of producing it. Manufacturer's profit after costs are deducted from his selling price.

Markets—When pertaining to a manufacturer's market, it refers to the places where his products are sold (a state, city, particular department store) and to a socio-economic class of purchasers.

Masonite—Inexpensive plywood board covered on one side with a pasted down rough canvas-like fabric.

Matte—Having a dull finish, not glossy.

Maxi—Word coined in 1968 for any skirt or coat length reaching the ankles.

Midi—See *Longuette.*

Mini—Originally a skirt length reaching to mid-thigh, or referring to any fashion item that is short.

Moiré—A stiff, heavy ribbed fabric, embossed to give a watered effect.

Mottled—Blotched in coloring.

Muslin—Plain weave cotton fabric, sheer to course, lustrous, washable, and long wearing.

Nap—On fabrics a fuzzy finish raised by brushing the surface.

No-run Colors—Fabric dyes that will not fade or run with washing.

Nylon—A strong, silky, washable, crease-, mildew- and moth-resistant man-made fiber.

Organdy—Sheer, high quality cotton fabric in open weave, made with permanent crispness.

Pellon—Trademark of Pellon Corp. for non-woven fabric used for interlining and made by fusing natural fibers and man-made fibers; and used as interlining in collars and facings, etc.

Pelt—The skin of an animal.

Permanent Press—All finishes on garments and fabrics that need no pressing, even after repeated washings.

Pile Weave—Weave with loops which produce a thick, soft surface. Loops may be left whole as in terry cloth, or cut, as in velvet, and the pile can be long or short, shaggy or smooth.

Placket—Word for slit at neck, side, front, back or wrist in dress, blouse, pants, or skirt to facilitate putting garment on. Buttons, zippers, snaps, etc. used for fastening.

Platinum—A very pale, silvery blond hair color.

Polyester—Man-made fibers which are shrink-proof and wrinkle- and moth-resistant. Yarns are knitted or woven, often in blended fabrics with cotton or rayon.

Price Range—The range or top and bottom price limits of a manufacturer's products. For example: The wholesale price range for a particular manufacturer's line of summer dresses is fifteen to twenty-five dollars.

Primary Colors—Red, blue, and yellow. These colors (plus white) are the basic colors from which all others are derived.

Production Costs—All the costs of producing a garment, from fabric to labor.

Ready-to-Wear—Apparel that is mass produced in standard sizes.

Retail Price—The price at which a garment is sold to the consumer; the department-store price as opposed to a wholesale price.

Rolled Hem—Narrow hem made by rolling the cut edge of fabric between the fingers to form a neat, tight edge, and sewing invisibly by hand. Used principally on scarves, bias-cut ruffles, and chiffon garments.

Rompers—Pants which are cut in one piece with the top of a garment.

Ruching—Trimming made by pleating a strip of lace, ribbon, net, muslin, etc., and stitching through the center.

Selvage—The narrow tightly woven finished band on either edge of fabric that prevents it from raveling.

Shade—A color with black added to it; i. e., a shade of blue.

Sheepskin Lining—The skin of a sheep dressed with the wool on it.

Size Groupings—Garments grouped according to a size such as 9 to 15.

Spandex—Man-made fibers that are stretchable, lightweight, and resistant to body acids. Used primarily for girdles, foundations, brassieres, and swimsuits.

Straight Grain—The direction of the warp or vertical threads of a fabric. Synonym for grainline.

Stretch Knits—Knit fabrics with a good deal of stretchability. Enough, for example, to pull a turtleneck collar over the head.

Style Trend—A fashion trend, such as long skirts, or an ethnic look.

Subcontractor—Someone who is contracted by a manufacturer to do the actual construction of the manufacturer's designs.

Sweater Knits—Knits used for sweaters. Bulkier yarn and looser stitches than in fabric knits.

Sweatshirt Fabric—Cotton knit with fleece backing, used for college sweatshirts and other sportswear.

Synthetic Fibers—Man-made fibers including acrylic, nylon, polyester, vinyl.

Tabard—A tunic with loose front and back panels. Popular style is tied on the side at the waistline.

Tailoring—Process of cutting, fitting, and finishing a garment to conform to the body by means of seams, darts, linings, pressing, etc. as in men's suits or coats; same techniques applied to women's suits, slacks, shirts, with simple clear lines, and no fancy details.

Tapered—Becoming gradually more slender and more fitted toward one end of the garment.

Three-dimensional—Having, or seeming to have, the quality of depth, as well as height and width.

Tint—A light tone of a color, with white added. In the case of water color paint, diluted with water.

Tone—The quality or character of a color.

Twill Weave—A fabric weave characterized by diagonal ribs, firm, and durable.

Ultrasuede—Trademark of Springs Mills for an imitation suede fabric which is durable, crease-resistant, and washable.

Value—The lightness or darkness of a color, its value.

Velour—A soft, thick pile fabric made in all cotton yarns, all wool yarns, or cotton and silk or mohair; used for coats and sportswear.

Warp—Basic weaving term for yarns in fabric that run parallel to selvage—the vertical threads.

Wash-and-wear—Requires no pressing even after repeated washings.

Weasel—Any small carnivorous animal belonging to the family *Mustelidae*.

Wholesale—Manufacturer's price to the retailer.

Woven Fabric—Made by interweaving the vertical, or warp, and horizontal, or filling, yarns on a loom, either by hand or machinery.

Yoke—Portion of garment across shoulders in front or back, usually a separate piece seamed to body of garment, and sometimes lined.

161

bibliography

Calasibetta, Charlotte. *Fairchild's Dictionary of Fashion*. New York: Fairchild Publications, 1975.

Davis, Marian L. *Visual Design in Dress*. Englewood Cliffs, N.J.: Prentice-Hall, Inc., 1980.

Jaffe, Hilde. *Children's Wear Design*. New York: Fairchild Publications, 1972.

Kopp, Ernestine, Vittorina Rolfo, Beatrice Zelin and Lee Gross. *Designing Apparel through the Flat Pattern,* Revised 5th edition. New York: Fairchild Publications, 1982.

Rosen, Selma. *Children's Clothing*. New York: Fairchild Publications, 1983.

Stephenson, Ann. *Introduction to Fashion Illustrating*. New York: Fairchild Publications, 1981.

Westerman, Maxine. *Elementary Fashion Design and Trade Sketching,* 2nd edition. New York: Fairchild Publications, 1983.

W and *Women's Wear Daily*. New York: Fairchild Publications.